T0355843

Praise for

ONE BOX *at a* TIME

"Sarah Williams is the definitive authority on subscription box businesses. With a track record of building a thriving seven-figure enterprise, Sarah's expertise shines through on every page of *One Box at a Time*. Her unwavering commitment to her craft is evident as she continues to actively engage in the industry, providing invaluable insights and guidance."

— **Dan Martell**, *Wall Street Journal* best-selling author of
Buy Back Your Time

"Sarah is the subscription box queen! *One Box at a Time* is an absolute gold mine of information and guidance. With its clarity, practicality, and real-world examples, this book is an invaluable tool for navigating the complexities of the rapidly growing subscription box industry."

— **Jennifer Allwood**, author of *Fear Is Not the Boss of You*

"Sarah has built raving communities from scratch, launched new companies, and taught others how to replicate her success. This book is a step-by-step guide to building your business, your passion, and yourself. If you're looking to start a subscription box, or any other type of business, this book is overflowing with tactical field-tested strategies that will save you months, if not years, of trial and error. My advice to you: take the leap."

— **Josh Band**, founder and CEO of Plate Crate

"*One Box at a Time* is a masterclass in crafting a successful subscription business. It's an authentic tapestry of hard-earned insights and actionable strategies, resonating with my own journey of creative exploration and growth. Consider this book your compass, guiding you from first step to fulfillment. A must-read for creators ready to design their business blueprint."

— **Bonnie Christine**, artist, fabric designer, and creative educator

"Whether you're an established brand with a recurring revenue model looking for that next edge or a first-time entrepreneur looking to enter the subscription market, *One Box at a Time* is the perfect read. This book is stuffed from cover to cover with actionable insights, hard-earned experience, and real-world advice."

— **Nathan Vazquez**, CEO of Pipsticks

HOW TO BUILD AND GROW
**A THRIVING SUBSCRIPTION
BOX BUSINESS**

SARAH WILLIAMS

HAY HOUSE, INC.
Carlsbad, California • New York City
London • Sydney • New Delhi

Published in the United States by: Hay House, Inc.: www.hayhouse.com®
Published in Australia by: Hay House Australia Pty. Ltd.: www.hayhouse
.com.au • *Published in the United Kingdom by:* Hay House UK, Ltd.: www
.hayhouse.co.uk • *Published in India by:* Hay House Publishers India: www
.hayhouse.co.in

Cover design: The Book Designers • *Interior design:* Nick C. Welch
Interior photos/illustrations: Alison Achieng

Library of Congress Cataloging-in-Publication Data

Names: Williams, Sarah (Subscription box coach), author.
Title: One box at a time : how to build and grow a thriving subscription
   box business / Sarah Williams.
Description: 1st edition. | Carlsbad, California : Hay House, Inc., [2023]
Identifiers: LCCN 2023026126 | ISBN 9781401974305 (hardback) | ISBN
   9781401974312 (ebook)
Subjects: LCSH: Subscription business. | New business enterprises.
Classification: LCC HF5417.6 .W56 2023 | DDC 658.1/1--dc23/eng/20230707
LC record available at https://lccn.loc.gov/2023026126

Hardcover ISBN: 978-1-4019-7430-5
E-book ISBN: 978-1-4019-7431-2
Audiobook ISBN: 978-1-4019-7432-9

10 9 8 7 6 5 4 3 2
1st edition, November 2023

Printed in the United States of America

SUSTAINABLE
FORESTRY
INITIATIVE

Certified Sourcing

www.forests.org
SFI-01268
SFI label applies to the text stock

*To the Launch Your Box community,
the fearless entrepreneurs who pour their hearts
into their small businesses, who pursue their
passions with relentless determination, who
create value and make a positive impact on their
communities—this book is dedicated to you. You
are the visionaries, the risk-takers, the makers and
doers who embody the spirit of entrepreneurship
and inspire us all to chase our dreams. May your
hard work, dedication, and love for what you do
continue to inspire and elevate those around you.*

CONTENTS

CONTENTS

FOREWORD

You're about to embark on an incredible journey of discovery that will forever change your business and, ultimately, your life. As someone who has been deeply entrenched in the membership and subscription world for more than 15 years, serving tens of thousands of different businesses in all kinds of markets, I can tell you that there is no better business model than recurring subscriptions.

You eliminate the stress and worry of where and when that next customer will appear and instead create the certainty of knowing exactly where your customers will be coming from, when they will be paying you, and how much will be coming in each month. This predictability enables you as a business owner to make decisions with a lot more confidence. You can hire with confidence, invest in your marketing with confidence, and have the certainty of knowing that you're never starting each month from zero. Your customers are compounding.

But it goes deeper than that. The health of this type of business boils down to two key factors: how many people join your subscription business and how many continue to stay. Because if your customers aren't happy, they'll cancel and leave (and that will happen). But a subscription business keeps us focused on what truly matters—keeping our customers happy. This is what forms a rewarding relationship with those you get to serve.

And that's why you're exactly where you need to be in reading this book from Sarah Williams. She knows how to keep her members happy (and paying). Yes, you will receive the specific strategies and tactical tips for creating a successful subscription box business. But more than that, you're going to discover the foundational insights into what it takes to keep customers happy and paying month after month.

I first met Sarah in 2018, when she became a student of mine. She then applied for my IMPACT mastermind (a group of high-level business owners focused on helping each other grow). At the time, her business was doing roughly $500K per year, with a mere 15 percent coming from her subscription boxes. The majority of revenue stemmed from her brick-and-mortar store. However, she could see that the future was in growing her subscription box business because it had scale far beyond her geographical location.

She was shy, reserved, and didn't say too much in the group. But she was a sponge . . . always showing up, always listening, and always taking notes. She soaked up everything—even though the online world was new to her and even though a lot of what we were discussing in the group wasn't directly relevant to her physical goods business.

In that situation, most people would think, "This isn't directly applicable to me," and quit. Not Sarah. She instead asked, "How could this apply to me?" That was the fundamental difference. Instead of focusing on what her business wasn't, Sarah chose to focus on what it could be, and over the next four years, we witnessed Sarah move from one strength to another with her business doubling, tripling, and beyond.

Her subscription business quickly grew from a local endeavor—where she would assemble her subscription boxes in the back of her store and subscribers would physically come to pick them up—to a big, new, beautiful warehouse with plenty of space, delivering thousands and thousands of subscription boxes each month all across the country.

But this was just the beginning. As her business took off, so did the number of people asking her how she was doing it. It wasn't long before Sarah realized she could help a lot more people by sharing her experience and knowledge of how to successfully grow a subscription box business.

It made sense, right? She had grown it from a few hundred local customers to thousands and thousands of customers nationwide. And this is when the true evolution of Sarah Williams began. Over the last few years, Sarah has taken her proven principles and shared them with tens of thousands of others, helping each of them launch their own subscription box businesses.

Through that, she's built a laboratory of best practices by gaining insight into the inner workings of the subscription box industry—well beyond just her own experience. From unique concepts to sourcing, packaging, and effective marketing strategies, there is nobody who has their finger on the pulse of the subscription box industry like Sarah.

Best of all, these strategies have proven to work across a wide variety of industries, from pet care to beauty products to single products like T-shirts, candles, socks, and so many more. Every single day she is working with people in hundreds of different niche markets, delivering thousands of different types of products in their subscription boxes.

That's what makes this book so unique. You're learning from someone who is not only doing what you want to do every day (run a successful subscription box business) but also someone who has intimate access to thousands of people running their own subscription box businesses. You not only get detailed insights from Sarah but you also get to tap into the collective wisdom of all the people Sarah is working with day in and day out.

So, yes, Sarah can tell you how to offset challenges that may arise along the way because she's likely faced those same challenges. From self-doubt and questions of "Who am I to be starting this kind of business?" to navigating the logistic challenges of figuring out how to ship items to hundreds (or thousands) of new subscribers after a successful launch. This isn't something she did years ago. It's something she is personally navigating every single day.

But more than that, Sarah gets to see new trends and best practices and understands what's working right now because of the tremendous community she has built of other subscription box business owners.

My advice is this: Like Sarah did years ago, as you read through this book, ask yourself the question, "How?" How might these strategies, tips, and insights apply to you? How could you start using what Sarah is sharing in each chapter within your business? And most important, how could you (no matter where you're starting from) begin today by applying what you're learning?

It doesn't matter if you are brand new to business or you're a name brand (like those that Sarah is now partnering with), what you're about to learn is powerful—and it works. Follow Sarah's teachings, apply what you learn, and take it one step at a time. If you do that, a year from now you'll be looking back on this moment with awe about how this one book has forever changed your life. Enjoy!

Stu McLaren
Co-founder, Searchie.io

AUTHOR'S NOTE

Throughout this book, I share resources and tools for how to build your subscription box business. I love giving you real-life, actionable steps, but we all know technology changes regularly. I tried to keep the references as helpful as possible. Since technology changes so often, you can find the most up-to-date resources on a separate website, SarahsBookBonus.com. I'll refer to this website throughout the book when it's relevant. There you can find additional training, downloads, webinars, graphics, and successful stories of other subscription box owners. You'll also find all the best and current tools to use.

INTRODUCTION

HOW MY SUBSCRIPTION BOX BUSINESS WAS BORN

When I was 21 years old, bright-eyed and fresh out of college, I went to work at a Fortune 500 company. It was a smart, safe decision that made sense. Every day I got up, went to the office, sat in my cubicle, and worked mostly with people who were twice my age (which is my age now). But soon I realized it was sucking the life out of me.

I was newly married, and my husband and I had been trying to conceive for a while, but it wasn't working. It was beginning to dawn on me that perhaps my life might not turn out exactly how I'd envisioned. *What if I never have children?* I thought. *What if I stay in this joyless job for another 10 years?* My whole life was in front of me, and this day-in and day-out grind was depressing.

I needed a change.

If I couldn't have children, I at least needed a career and environment I enjoyed and to create a better life for myself. So I decided to go back to school to be an architect. For two years I got up early in the morning and stayed up late at night, learning color theory, drawing, and painting, and letting my creative heart run wild. I had never considered myself creative before, but I was great at drawing and painting freehand.

I enrolled in additional classes at my local art studio in my tiny Texas hometown. Multiple days of the week after work, I took tons of those "sip and paint" classes, where people drink wine and learn how to paint a specific picture. I loved chatting with all the women taking the classes. Soon I began helping out with paint supplies and cleanup while the instructors taught. Eventually the classes expanded from 10 to 40 participants regularly. They were always sold out, but I had befriended the owner and could get in whenever I wanted.

Eventually, I dropped out of art school entirely. To my surprise, when I finished the fundamental art classes and did get to those design classes, they involved a fair amount of math, which I didn't like at all. I had already lost interest in anything except the art classes, plus I was pregnant. Then one afternoon, the owner of my local art studio called me and said, "Sarah, I'm so, so sick and have a huge class tonight. I hate to ask, but could you sub in for me tonight?"

Me? Teach? I'd never taught anything in my life. "It's the same painting we did last week," she went on. "You already know how to do it." But still, I was scared. I wasn't an "up in front of people" kind of person. I was about to say no when she said, "I'll pay you $400." Sold.

Teaching the class that night wasn't perfect, but it was the first time I had made money doing something I liked, and it wasn't long before they offered me a full-time job. And this was the catalyst for everything that followed.

I noticed that my students would create these beautiful paintings they wanted to display but always complained that the only places in town to have them framed cost upward of $80.

That's ridiculous, I thought. *I bet I can make frames myself easily enough.* And so I began making frames for my students and selling them for $40 a piece at the end of each class. The colors matched the paintings each night, and I set them up in the studio every time I taught. But frames soon took over my house.

At the end of that year, a friend had to back out of an art booth she bought for a huge trade show called Christmas Magic, and she offered it to me. It was a giant show with the potential for big business, and I was psyched. By the end of that show, I had made thousands of dollars in just 48 hours. *I can do this*, I thought, maybe for the first time. Plus now I had a little capital to get my own business up and running.

Riding high off that win, I quit the art studio and rented a tiny 600-foot studio right in the heart of town. Actually, more honestly, I had a good friend who owned the salon next door to the studio, and she set up an appointment with the property owner and just about forced me into it. I'm not sure I would have had the courage to go for it if it wasn't for her. Three hundred of those square feet made up a cute little storefront for the frames, and the other 300 were behind a wall and provided a work and art class space for me.

One day, a woman came in with a basic silver Yeti cup and asked if I could monogram it for her. "My husband and I are always mixing ours up," she said. I'm from Texas and live for a monogram, so I created one on vinyl for her cup, and she loved it. Pretty soon, I began monogramming anything anyone brought me. I got a wholesale license and started selling the Yetis and other products in the store. Eventually that little shop of mine upgraded into a much bigger, more collaborative 4,000-square-foot shop that partnered with other local boutiques.

But I still had a problem. After I posted new product pictures and videos on social media, we'd sell out instantly. When my tried-and-true people who'd been with me since the beginning came to the store days later, the product would already be gone. I felt terrible . . . but I thought I might have a solution.

The idea for a subscription box was planted in my mind years before, when I saw a big company doing a monthly monogram box (and y'all already know how I feel about a monogram). I thought a subscription box might be a good way to help my VIP customers feel valued and excited and ensure they received all the best stuff. But it felt too hard, too complicated. That company probably had hundreds of thousands of subscribers, so I wasn't sure if little ole me could pull it off. I was already overwhelmed. So that idea just lingered.

But one day, I was wrapping up a meeting with my web developer when he asked, "Is there anything else I can do for you?"

I hadn't planned on it, but suddenly I blurted out, "I want to do a subscription box. Can you help me figure out the logistics?"

"Sure," he said. We talked through how to set up recurring monthly payments and how to create an order page on the website. "I can have this ready for you by March."

Three months! I had ninetyish days to figure out how to curate and run a subscription box program. I felt a little regret, but my developer was already working on it and I'd committed. It's like opening a can of biscuits—you can't put them back in the can—so here went nothing.

I set a goal of getting 50 people to sign up for that first box. Fifty just felt like a good, round number—not too high, but high enough to justify the idea. Researching began, and I decided what to put in each box and how to package them. The products I picked for that first box were bestsellers in my store with a brand-new design. They included a stainless-steel tumbler, a monogrammed cosmetic bag, and phone charger wraps all in the same color palette. I purchased 50 of everything and set the price at $40.

By March, I was ready to go and announced on Facebook that I was starting a subscription box. I didn't know anything about marketing or ads—I just lobbed it out on social media to my loyal, local following from the shop. I wanted everything in the box to be a surprise, so I just promised them that if they loved my shop, they'd love this box. I intimately knew my customers. I had been serving them long enough that I knew I could make good on that promise.

Before the first boxes were ready, 44 people subscribed. It wasn't 50, but I was thrilled. Everything I did was still local, so people had to either come to the shop for pickup or I hand-delivered a few of them. That first day, people were already waiting in line for the shop to open before I arrived. Seeing their reactions as they opened the boxes was the coolest experience. They loved getting a surprise gift that felt like it was made just for them, because it was. The love I have for those original customers is something special that sticks with me still and continues to fuel everything I do today.

The next month I planned for 75 boxes and even began a waiting list when those sold out. The month after that I did 100, and by the end of the year I had over 300 subscribers. I was hooked. Thinking through what I would put in my boxes to my most loyal and beloved customers became my favorite part of the business. Plus I was beginning to realize the tremendous advantage of predictable, regularly recurring income, which in retail is hard to come by.

Pretty soon, I saw the number of out-of-town buyers in my customer base grow. First there was one subscriber in Utah, and then within a couple months, there were eight as she told her friends and word spread organically. Within three years, I had over 600 subscribers, and subscription boxes had taken over every inch of the workroom where I taught classes.

During this time, I had two children. It took six years, but my husband and I eventually had a son and a daughter, and their lives were also taking over our own in the best way. School plays, soccer games, homework, meetings, playdates, and tournaments meant that I couldn't always be at the store anymore. I needed flexibility. I wanted to be able to attend everything for my kids and be the kind of mom I dreamed of for so long. The subscription box business was booming. Online sales were already outperform-. ing our brick-and-mortar business, and I had a hunch that with my full effort it could be even bigger. So I decided to stop teaching art classes.

I wasn't completely ready to close the shop, though, because for years it was my main focus and the beginning of the beautiful relationship I had with all of my customers. And then, the COVID pandemic arrived, and I didn't have much of a choice.

I was determined to not lay off any of my employees. At first, selling during the pandemic felt icky. Jumping on Facebook live and saying, "Hey, come buy this cute

T-shirt," while people were literally dying out there was just weird.

But I kept showing up, and our subscriptions continued to grow. I started to hear from people that our boxes were such a bright spot in a dark time. Everyone wanted something to look forward to. I curated the boxes specifically to be even more hopeful and inspirational than usual. People couldn't go shopping, so I went shopping for them. We posted pictures of me and my employees packaging T-shirts on our living room floors with our kids running around. *We're real people too, just trying to keep going.*

Within the next couple years, the world was through the worst of the pandemic. I did reopen the store for a little while, but it was never the same, and eventually we closed for good and moved the business entirely online. Today, I have thousands of subscribers.

IF I CAN DO IT, SO CAN YOU

After the subscription box business took off, people began to regularly ask how they could start their own. "Could we get coffee? Can I pick your brain?" people messaged me. Finally, I obliged and helped my first client obtain over 100 subscribers in her first month of business. That's when it dawned on me—this is replicable. I'm a small-town mom who's made every mistake in the book but still managed to create a seven-figure business creating monthly gifts for people. If I can do it, so can anyone else.

That's exactly what I'm going to teach you here. You don't need to know anything yet about running a subscription box business. All you need is the desire to learn and a willingness to serve your customers. Starting my subscription box business was life-changing for me, and it can be for you. Here's how:

1. **Predictable, recurring monthly income.** Unless you go get a "regular" job, this is hard to come by in the entrepreneurial world. Before I had my subscription box, I enjoyed running my own business and being my own boss, but the stress of irregular income was tough. When the pandemic hit, the money from my subscription box business sustained my entire family and all of our employees for months. Lots of my students do this for extra income, but for some of them, like me, this box business has become their livelihood.

2. **Freedom to work whenever and wherever you want.** Almost all of my students have families and busy lives. This model of business allows them to not only provide for themselves and their families but also be there for the most important moments.

3. **The most fun way to do business.** A subscription box is basically a box full of gifts for your friends! Sure, you might not know them personally, but you share common interests, and you want to serve them. (That said, I will teach you how to research your customer so well you might actually feel like you do know them.) Every month you get to pick out goodies to make your subscribers feel happy, even loved. It's so cool and an absolute blast.

In the next 10 chapters, I'll take you from having zero ideas or platforms to curating your first box and gaining your first customers. We'll also cover how to keep growing your business, if that's what you want to do. Money isn't everything. Believe me, I know that. But it sure does make life easier. Providing for yourself and your family is a worthwhile goal. Building this business isn't something you need to starve for. You can make a legitimate business off a subscription box. You can do it as a side hustle or turn it into a full-time career. If you already have a business, like I did when I started my subscription, this could be another lucrative income stream and way to serve your customers. Whatever success looks like for you in this world, I want to help you build and grow a subscription box business that supports the life you want.

We'll cover:

- Determining your ideal customer
- Building community
- Curating products
- Launching your box
- Growing beyond it

But don't be overwhelmed; we'll take it one step at a time. I'll also continue to share parts of my story along the way and teach you everything you need to know to make this dream of yours a reality.

My students have gone on to create thriving subscription box businesses, many of whom I'll introduce you to here. Some of them serve niches you couldn't even imagine! From female dentists to guinea pig lovers to miniature-jigsaw-puzzle enthusiasts, a subscription box business can work for almost any audience if you do it right. There is a place for anyone who wants to create a business like this—one that supports the life you want to live and brings joy to your customers. I'll show you how. Come on, let's dive in!

Chapter 1

COMMIT TO SHOW UP

My phone beeped and the message flashed on the screen. "Where are you?" my virtual assistant texted from several states away. She was waiting for me to go live on my Facebook page. We'd been planning this for a long time. Our subscribers had just received their boxes, and it was time for me to open one live on camera to help get everyone excited and hopefully gain new subscribers, as those who didn't get a box this time saw what they were missing.

Everything was ready. My mannequins were dressed and posed, ready to show off my supercute new products—products I knew my audience loved. I even knew exactly what I wanted to say, and I'd written out notes to make sure I didn't forget anything. I'd had my hair done because I knew that if my hair looked good, I'd feel good.

My laptop was expertly placed to capture the best angle of my face and showcase the most inviting view of the store. I had done this many times before! I knew it was helpful for people to hear me talk about the products, style them, and discuss different ways to use them in their life. I had showed them my top five things to take on a road trip or what you need to transition your wardrobe from summer to fall. For my first couple videos a year earlier, no one showed up, which was both a relief and a disappointment. I had been dreading it so much that it almost felt like a gift when no one was there.

But I'd done all that prep work to get ready, and it felt bad to waste all that time. So I showed up anyway. And I kept showing up day after day, even when no one else did and it felt pointless. Eventually, it started to feel like what I did every day when I connected with people in my store, natural even. Soon, the few people watching began asking questions in the comments, and slowly engagement grew. I watched the numbers slowly climb from 0 to 20 to 50. And one Saturday morning more than 100 people joined me live. That day I freaked out a little and wanted to vomit when I saw that many people, but I was already live, so I powered through.

But this particular day, with my assistant frantically texting and probably afraid something had happened to me and the clock marking 10 minutes past when I was scheduled to be on, I couldn't push the button to go live on my business's social media page. My legs shook. My breath came in shallow gasps. My armpits and palms started sweating. I felt my face getting hot. My phone beeped again. "Sarah, where are you?" my assistant texted a second time.

Remember my awesome subscription box success story, when I launched that first month with 44 subscribers, then hit 100 subscribers in three months and 300 in nine months? Well, it was incredible. I felt invincible. It was one of the most exciting times in my business. Until it wasn't. I had planned for more growth after that first year. But I hit a plateau. I had 300 subscribers, but I couldn't

seem to move beyond that. Even worse, with the occa-
sional cancellations that are part of any subscription box
business, within a few months my numbers even began
to shrink!

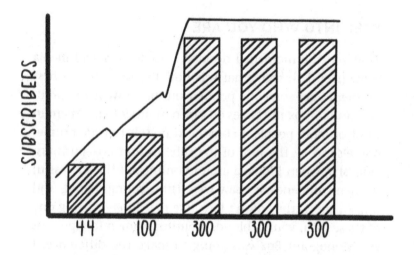

I tried not to panic. I'd ordered products months in
advance because that's what you have to do when you
order by the hundreds. But I had inventory piling up on
my shelves and a lot of money invested in product that
wasn't selling. Ten unsold boxes turned into 50, and it
kept increasing from there. All that product was just sitting there costing me money. Most of my business was
still local, and my town is small. There are only so many
people in the same town who can wear the same shirt,
right? At some point, this was bound to happen. I had to
do something. . . .

I needed a bigger pool. I knew out-of-town subscribers
would be the key to my continued growth. What I didn't
know was how to find them, connect with them, and make
them part of my subscriber community. Other business

owners I knew were blowing up because they were doing lots of live video. I had tried to grow every other possible way I could think of, but it wasn't working. But why would anyone want to see more of me?

STEP INTO WHO YOU ARE

That was the moment I decided I needed a social media influencer. I thought that was how to grow my business online: to get someone popular online to wear my products and unbox my boxes on video in order to get them in front of more people. I convinced myself I needed someone else to be the face of my subscription box business. Honestly, when I looked around online, all the successful women (influencers) I saw were thin, young, blond, and tan. In short, they didn't look like me. Surely getting one of these thin, young, blond, beautiful women to represent my Monogram Box was going to make the difference. I convinced myself that that was the missing piece. If only I could find the right influencer, my business would start to grow again.

In addition to my quest for the perfect Instagram model to represent my business, I decided to join a mastermind group and attend our first in-person retreat in California. I'd been excited to go, but once I arrived, I was filled with feelings of self-doubt and intimidation. The other people in the mastermind were big earners. Most of them were multi-seven-figure earners, and I was making only six figures, nowhere near that. When I heard them talk about their businesses, I wondered why I'd even applied. *This was a huge mistake*, I thought.

That first day I was so nervous I hid in the back of the room, trying not to get noticed. The longer I sat in that room, the more the feelings of self-doubt grew. I didn't even know what the other people were talking about. I kept writing down terms they used so I could google them when I returned to my room. I felt so out of place, so unworthy of being there, that I started looking for flights home that night. I was sure I was in the wrong place. I called one of my business friends and cried. I told her I didn't belong at the retreat, that my business was too small, and I wasn't successful enough to be there.

We were all staying in one big rental house, and my talking and crying were louder than I thought, because one of the other women in the mastermind overheard me. Soon she knocked on my door and talked to me about how I was feeling. There was no hiding it now, so I was honest with her.

"I don't belong here," I said.

She was kind and said, "Yes, you do. Your business is booming, and you have knowledge the rest of us don't have. You do belong here."

After a while she was able to talk me out of leaving, but I still didn't want to do my "hot seat" that was scheduled for the next day. A hot seat is when you ask a specific question in front of the group and everyone attempts to answer and give you feedback. Having successful business owners give you feedback about something you're working on in your business is a great concept, but the thought of all eyes in the room being on me and appearing incompetent was too much to bear.

I talked to my mentor, who ran the mastermind, and he said, kindly, that I wasn't getting out of the hot seat, but he suggested I go first so I didn't have to worry about it all day. At least there wouldn't be a missing person's report when I snuck out of the room and ran for home before it was my turn. I'd get it over with and be able to relax instead of dwelling on it. It still didn't sound great, but I did come all that way, after all. Plus I still wanted to know how to get influencers to promote my business. Surely this group knew how to accomplish that.

I was filled with anxiety as I stood in front of the group and asked them the question I'd struggled with for months: How could I take this amazingly successful local business and turn it into an online business while maintaining the same meaningful connection I have with local customers? Then I asked if any of them worked with influencers or brand ambassadors. "I think that's what I need to reach more out-of-town customers," I said. "I need someone cool and influential to promote my business."

The other members of the mastermind didn't answer my questions outright. Instead, they asked me questions about my business and my customers—and they asked questions about *me*. What made my business so special? Why had I been so successful up until now? How do I decide what to put in a box? Who are my customers? The answers came easy to me. I had been successful because I knew my customers inside and out. I'd sold to them, and we'd chatted countless times in the store. Plus I deeply cared about them. I wanted them to feel important and loved when they opened their boxes. I was passionate about serving them. And, because I knew them, I let them know me. As I answered my fellow mastermind members, it hit me: I was the influencer of my business.

The people I wanted to serve with my subscription box—to surprise and delight with things I knew they'd love month after month—were just like me. They were busy Southern moms, running around trying to do all the things. These women spent their days doing things for others, taking care of everyone else. They rarely took the time to do anything special for themselves, so I wanted to do special things for them. It was these women, who were just like me, that I wanted to serve.

And they didn't want to watch someone thin, young, blond, and perfectly tan tell them about my products. They wanted me to tell them. They related to me. They saw themselves in me. I sold more large and extra-large T-shirts (my size) than any other size. My audience didn't want to see how my T-shirts looked on someone thin and young and "perfect." They wanted to see them on me. They wanted to see that my products looked cute on me—someone who looked a lot like them.

I went home from that retreat encouraged that I had the answer to my problem but nervous that now I had to be the influencer for my business. The reason I'd hit that plateau with my subscription box was that I'd tapped out my local market. But there was something else: those subscribers sitting in other parts of the country beyond my little town who I just knew would love my subscription box didn't know *me*. And now that I wasn't going to hire an influencer to be the face of my brand, I had to show up, fully myself.

I thought about my customers and why they kept returning to my shop. Sure, they liked the on-trend, personalized clothing, accessories, and gift items I sold in my store. But it was more than that. I talked with every person who came into the store. I greeted them, and we chatted about what was going on in their lives. My regular customers became more than just customers. They became friends. I took the time and made the effort to connect with them and build relationships with them.

It was that connection that was missing with my online audience. In order to grow, I needed to let them get to know me. Simply offering my products in the online shop and waiting for people to buy wasn't going to be enough. I needed to show up for my online customers the same way I showed up for the customers who came into my physical store. In order to grow my business, I needed to become visible online. It's a small thing, but I had never said "y'all" on social media because I thought that made me sound like I wasn't smart, even though I say it in person all the time. Then I realized my customers are Southern and they say "y'all" too. Fully letting down my guard to strangers on the Internet felt super scary . . . maybe I could just start with saying "y'all?"

I needed to show up for my online customers the same way I showed up for the customers who came into my physical store.

It came down to fear of the unknown. Putting myself out there online felt different than meeting new people face-to-face. If I had a room full of new students who had never come to a painting workshop before, I could see their reactions. I was able to see where they were getting stuck; I could read their body language and facial expressions. Showing up on camera where I couldn't see anyone on the other side watching me felt very uncomfortable. It was no longer a familiar setting. It felt like uncharted territory, and I wasn't sure I could do it.

The fear was big, but the desire to see my subscription box business grow was bigger. I knew it could be special.

I knew it mattered to the women who were subscribers, and it would matter to those future subscribers who just needed to get to know me and what I had to offer, which brings me back to that day in the shop, with my assistant pinging me, my hair done and palms sweating, desperately trying to push the button. Finally, I did it. I started to accept my role as the influencer of my business and went live. It was a little anticlimactic. I'd love to tell you that right from the start these videos were brilliant, and I discovered a true love for being on camera. Instead, like everything else in business, it was a process.

The fear was big, but the desire to see my subscription box business grow was bigger.

But I kept going live and started to reach more people outside of my area. They got to know me and my personality. They either related to me or they didn't, and I accepted that. They either followed and bought from me or they didn't. I learned to be okay with that too. I reminded myself that I wasn't for everyone. I would attract people who were like me and needed to stop worrying about everyone else. Soon I was gaining new subscribers again. I hit 600 within the next few months, then 1,000 a few months after that. I managed my growth and all the challenges that came with it. I still go live with my audience consistently, showing up and talking about my products. They love to engage with me in the comments, and we get to know each other, making connections and building relationships. I show up for my audience, connect with them, and have fun with them. And that has made all the difference.

I reminded myself that I wasn't for everyone.

BELIEVE IN YOURSELF

This chapter isn't actually about going live on social media. That's a helpful strategy, and we'll cover it in a later chapter, so don't worry about that now. But it *is* about showing up. I'll never forget the day that I sat in my office, shaking and sweating, desperately trying to think of a reason *not* to push the button—the first time going live fully as myself, trying to reach new people. I can instantly put myself back in that chair, feeling all those feelings. Then I remember what I realized during that mastermind: there wasn't anyone else who could do this better than me. I was my business and my audience wanted me, just as I am.

In building your own subscription box business, you will face similar moments of self-doubt. There is no way around it. You will be scared, embarrassed, hesitant, anxious, or even panicked. And sometimes even for good reason. But starting a business isn't just about knowing your customers; it's about showing up and *letting them know you*. Before we get into the technical nitty-gritty of everything I know you want to learn, you must first learn these few truths:

1. **You can trust yourself.** Many times in your entrepreneurial journey, you won't know what to do. You'll hit a roadblock—a tech problem, pricing decision, social media mess up—and you might even make one or two big mistakes. Trust that you will figure it out. You will not know every answer ahead of time. That's okay. Trust yourself that if you keep taking the next step, the road will reveal itself. Trust that when you make a mistake, you can fix it. I was terrified to go live in front of strangers; I didn't know what would happen or what came next. But I trusted myself to handle it.

2. **You have to show up.** Showing up, completely as you are, even when you don't want to, is an essential part of building your business. Just like me, at some point you will be sweaty and nauseous (maybe even now!) as you take a step toward building your dreams. Take the step anyway. If it doesn't challenge you, it won't change you.

3. **You are enough.** Each one of you. I have since started my own mastermind group and regularly see my talented, creative students serving and connecting with their customers, making a difference in their lives. It's like magic watching them work. They're taking a chance on themselves, bringing an idea to the world. And yet they still doubt themselves. They struggle with feeling like they can do this. I'll admit, I still feel this way sometimes at big pivotal moments in my business, like when I added a coaching business, became a public speaker, and started a mastermind. But the important thing is that you feel those feelings and still push the damn button anyway, whatever that means to you. Go live, create the website, step on stage, buy the product, talk to someone, read the book, do the thing.

If it doesn't challenge you,
it won't change you.

I believe in you. You can borrow my belief if you need it. Before we go any further, I need you to commit to me and to yourself that you're going to trust yourself, show up, and believe you are enough, even when it's hard. Okay then, let's keep moving.

Action Steps

1. Identify what is holding you back from showing up. I am introverted, and the thought of talking in front of people I didn't know was enough to make me shut down. Plus I didn't like the way I looked, which didn't help.

2. Do something to help you overcome what you've identified in action step number 1. I started getting my hair done and asking my friends to show up for me when I went live so it felt like a safe space for me.

3. Challenge yourself. Set a date and time to do something new and challenging, and make sure someone is there to hold you accountable. It will get easier. I promise.

Chapter 2

DETERMINE YOUR IDEAL CUSTOMER

Amanda Stucky is a planner junkie. Maybe you know the type—the kind of person who has eight different pens, stickers for every occasion, and notebooks everywhere. But Amanda's planner obsession is quite specific. She is a devoted fan of a planner called the Hobonichi. It's a Japanese calendar/planner that can be customized in countless ways and whose popularity has spread to the U.S. One quick Google search and you'll discover these graph-paper-looking planners have a cult-like following. Amanda is one of these followers. There's a whole ecosystem around Hobonichi planners that even includes specific kinds of fountain pens because of the unique paper the planners are made of. A lover of beautiful and creative things, Amanda likes to use cute stickers in her planners but was unable to find any that fit the unique specifications of the Hobonichi. She bought stickers made for a different brand of planner, applied them to hers, and used an X-Acto knife and ruler to cut them to fit perfectly.

For fun, she began creating weekly "Plan with Me" videos on YouTube specifically for others who enjoyed the Hobonichi. People subscribed to her channel not only to follow along with her in their own planners but also to connect with Amanda, as she talked about her upcoming week and what was going on in her life. Over time, she built a community of regular visitors, building relationships with them and serving them helpful information about how she uses her planner. When she floated the idea of making her own stickers to her community, they responded enthusiastically. First she created one-time-purchase sticker packs. Those regularly sold out, so she knew she could do more. As luck would have it, a woman in a Facebook group they both belonged to told her she really should start a subscription box and sent her my way. Amanda was intimidated, but she believed in her idea and the predictable monthly income was enticing. With the income she already made, they were pretty close to enabling her husband to quit his job to be home more, which was "the big, scary goal" for their family. So, she decided to go for it—to create a subscription box for Hobonichi enthusiasts to receive her cute, functional stickers every month.

She purchased enough materials to curate 100 boxes that first month, priced at $29. She didn't want to be left with too much excess inventory if the launch didn't go as well as she hoped. It turns out, she didn't need to worry about that at all. When Amanda launched to her YouTube audience of 600 people, she sold out of those 100 boxes immediately. And her success only grew from there. Today, Amanda has multiple kinds of planner sticker boxes with hundreds of subscribers. She also has hundreds of thousands of views on her YouTube videos showing the different types of Hobonichi planners, which ones to choose, and how to use them. And, drumroll please . . .

her husband did get to quit his full-time engineering job to do behind-the-scenes work with Amanda. All because of stickers made specifically for a planner most of you haven't even heard of before! Are you paying attention yet, friends? This is possible for anyone.

IDENTIFY YOUR IDEAL CUSTOMER

Let's examine Amanda's success for a minute. When she launched her first box, even her first product, she didn't launch to just anyone. She launched to 600 devoted fans of the same specific planner that Amanda loves and wants to accessorize. They are what we call her *ideal customer.* This is the person for whom your subscription box either delights with something they want or solves a problem with something they need. Sometimes both. Your ideal customer is the person who gets the most value from your offer, and in return, you get the most value from having them as your customer. Amanda is crystal clear on who her subscription box is for and what that person wants and needs. Her product is for creative women who love and use Hobonichi planners regularly. Before you start your own subscription box business, you need to identify your own ideal customer. You need to ask yourself, "Who am I for?"

When I decided to add a subscription box to my business, I already knew my ideal customer. She had been shopping with me for years. My gift shop became known as the place to come for personalized gifts and on-trend graphic tees and accessories, and I had many regular customers who shopped with me at least once a month. It was those customers who became my first subscribers. They were the women I thought about as I was dreaming about my own subscription box. My ideal customer is a busy Southern mom. She doesn't have time to spend doing something special for herself because she is too busy taking care of everyone else. She likes cute, trendy clothes and accessories, but she doesn't have the time or energy to spend choosing them and putting outfits together herself. I have a desire to treat that busy Southern mom to something just for her. And it has to be monogrammed. In the South we say, "If it isn't monogrammed, is it even really yours?" Reese Witherspoon once echoed, "My rule is, if it's not moving, monogram it." I want you all to build thriving subscription box businesses, but a lofty secondary goal might be to get you all on the monogram train. Anyway, I knew if I curated a subscription box filled with cute, trendy personalized T-shirts and accessory items, my ideal customer would love it.

I knew it because, basically, I am her.

That makes it pretty easy, right? One of the best pieces of advice I give my students is to serve people exactly like you. It's the best way to know how to speak directly to and understand your customer. My boxes are so curated to my taste, you could probably easily guess what my favorite colors are just by looking over what I regularly send.

If you aren't passionate and deeply knowledgeable about your ideal customer, you won't connect with them.

Your ideal customer doesn't have to be you, but it's more likely that they will be. It just makes sense. We're drawn to the things we enjoy. But the most important thing is that you are absolutely passionate about these people and the products you're selling. If you aren't passionate and deeply knowledgeable about your ideal customer, you won't connect with them. Or perhaps, even worse, you might connect well enough, but you'll soon burn out and hate what you're doing. I've seen this a couple times in my membership, when someone tries to start a subscription box business for an audience they don't know well enough. If you want to sell men's bow ties, but you're a woman who doesn't know much about men's style, behavior, or wants or needs in that area, you won't be able to speak their language. And to put it bluntly, your business will struggle.

Lean in to who you are and the communities you know. You might not be a teenage girl, but perhaps you've been teaching them for 10 years or have one of your own. When you truly know your ideal customer—when you understand what they're doing, thinking, and feeling— you're able to do everything better. You choose items for your box with the confidence that comes from knowing your ideal customer will love them. Your messaging is on point because you speak your ideal customer's language and use that language in everything from social media posts to e-mails and website copy. And best of all, you're all but guaranteed success because when you understand your customer, all you have to do is give them what they want.

THE RICHES ARE IN THE NICHES

In the subscription box industry, a niche is a small part of the market with well-defined wants, interests, or needs. While some subscription box owners worry that a small part of the market means a small opportunity for success, as you learned from Amanda's story, the opposite is actually true. A mistake many subscription box hopefuls make is trying to keep their audiences too broad. There is a fear that by narrowing down, they'll limit the pool of potential subscribers. "The riches are in the niches" isn't just a catchy saying, it's something I teach and believe every day. If you try to speak to everyone, you end up speaking to no one. Going too broad with your audience means you're unable to reach anyone with your messaging. A broad audience leads to messaging that speaks in generalities, lacking the personal touch that creates the oh-so-necessary connections (and subscription sign-ups).

You and your products aren't for everyone, and that's okay. In fact, that's better than okay; it's great! Knowing who you're *not* for is just as important as knowing who you *are* for. It's time to lean in to that self-confidence we talked about in the last chapter. Be okay with people not subscribing to your box, because you are so clear on who you do serve that you know those people will subscribe when they find you. And when people pass you by, bless them and let them go on their merry way. Not everyone loves monograms, I know that (as much as I don't understand it). Those people likely are not my ideal customer and I'm okay with that. I'll still be out here selling leopard-print monograms, waiting for my ideal Southern moms to find me. Because when they do, they won't just think, "Oh, that's nice." They'll think, "Wow! That was made just for me!" When you niche down and get really specific about who your ideal customer is, you're able to serve them better.

2 STEPS TO KNOWING YOUR AUDIENCE

Now it's time to figure out who you *are* for. There are two important steps in this process. Let's get tactical.

Step 1: Define Your Ideal Customer

First, let's think through the demographics of your ideal customer. These descriptors will be more of the obvious things like gender, age, profession, interests, and so on. Answer these questions to help guide your thinking:

- Is your ideal customer a man or a woman?
- Are they an adult or a child?
- Do they have children? If so, what age(s) are they?
- What are their hobbies?
- What are their interests?
- What is their profession?
- How old are they?
- What books do they read? What shows do they watch? What music do they listen to?
- Where do they shop / what are their favorite brands?

Thinking through these questions helps you start to develop a clear picture of the ideal customer for your subscription box. Take your time here and put effort into getting really specific. Defining your ideal customer makes every aspect of starting and launching your subscription box easier and more effective.

Step 2: Get to Know Your Ideal Customer

Next let's think through the psychographics of your ideal customer. These are a bit deeper and describe people's attitudes, feelings, and aspirations. Think through questions like:

- What daily struggles do your ideal customers have?
- What are their fears?
- What are their goals?
- What do they wish were different?
- What makes them happy?
- What are their values?

If you have trouble answering these questions off the top of your head, do some research. Head to some Facebook groups or Reddit pages. Look at Amazon reviews of products your ideal customer might use or even just ask people on social media or in real life. Anything you can think of to get into the mind of your ideal customers is time well spent.

Often my students will think they've niched down, but I have to challenge them to niche again. Don't be afraid to get specific. It will pay off in the long run. Let's say a new subscription box owner has an idea for a box. She has identified her target audience as teenage girls—all teenage girls. If you spend any time at all with teenage girls, you know how varied their interests, personalities, and challenges can be. I'd ask this subscription box owner to get more specific. Here are some ways to consider niching down further:

- Teenage girls interested in pursuing a future in STEM-related fields
- Teenage girls dealing with anxiety
- Teenage girls who are high-level competitive athletes
- Teenage girls who love to knit
- Teenage girls who are passionate about musical theater

Each of these groups of girls has different needs and interests. And there are still plenty of them out there to create enough of an audience to support a subscription box. Imagine how specific a subscription box owner could get with her messaging if she were talking to female high school students who play competitive soccer. She could speak directly to the challenges of balancing school and soccer, the mental toll a highly competitive environment can take on teenage girls, and the need to protect themselves from injury, among other things. The result is an ideal customer who feels heard and understood.

Maybe a new subscription box owner decides to start a box for teachers. That sounds pretty specific, right? Not quite. We can do better than that. Consider these:

- Elementary school teachers
- Special education teachers
- Reading teachers
- High school math teachers
- Teachers who are into style
- Teachers who live in the South
- Teachers who are mothers
- Teachers who love organization

You can imagine that messaging that speaks to a preschool teacher is quite different from messaging that speaks to a high school science teacher. Preschoolers and high school students have different needs, problems, and interests, and so do the people who teach them. Creating messaging and curating products that speak to that ideal customer becomes simple when you know exactly who that person is and what they want.

A SMALL NICHE WITH BIG RESULTS

Anne Stuccio is another one of my students who serves her small niche incredibly well. She's not your typical subscription box owner—Anne is a practicing dentist with more than 20 years of experience. Although she's a successful dentist with a thriving practice, Anne had never sold anything online. But only six months after launching her subscription box, she was bringing in over $10,000 in recurring revenue. She was able to reach that level of success so quickly while practicing dentistry full time for one reason: she went super specific with her niche. Anne's The Brighter Life for Dentists box is exclusively for female dentists.

I love the story behind Anne's box. Anne had never thought of starting a subscription box. Why would she? She was a practicing dentist with a busy practice. She was also a wife and mother. The last thing she was looking for was something to fill the spare time she didn't have. Still, you never know where you'll find inspiration or what that inspiration will lead to. For Anne, the idea for her box was born inside of a Facebook group for female dentists. There were more than 8,000 members of the group, and Anne noticed so many of them talking about the same challenges.

They struggled with feelings of exhaustion, overwhelm, and burnout, as they found themselves constantly placing others' needs ahead of their own. Simply put, they weren't enjoying practicing dentistry the way they once had. Anne related strongly to these women, the women who would become her ideal customers, because she was one of them. She also struggled with the stresses of being a working mom and trying to get it all done, balancing her many household management duties with the stress of being a clinician in charge of a sizable staff in her dental practice.

She wanted to support these women. She wanted to create something that would help them rediscover and reignite their love for dentistry. Anne joined my membership, Launch Your Box, and filled her boxes with things to make her subscribers feel supported, nurtured, encouraged, and inspired. What to send her subscribers was easy because she understood their challenges and obstacles so well. Inspired by her new mission, Anne took charge and made things happen. She figured out all the things and launched her subscription box quickly. Her launch was so successful that she sold out during her first launch, and she continues to grow her six-figure subscription box business to this day. She even has monthly themes like #DentalBossBabe and #MySweetTooth. Goodies in her boxes have included everything from baseball hats to dental humor, cute desk objects to soothing candles.

The first step in creating the subscription box business of your dreams is knowing who you are for. Your ideal customers are out there just waiting to be served by you. You have something unique and amazing to offer a small subset of people. Define who they are, and everything you do will feel like it was created just for them. Every month I get to create a box filled with things I know my subscribers will love. I provide them with something functional, because we're moms and we need to get stuff done; something fun, because it's important to remember to keep the fun in our days no matter how busy they are; and something special that they wouldn't buy for themselves. I know what they think, feel, and do, because I took the time to learn about them. In the next chapter we're going to work on building an audience and finding these exact ideal customers.

Your ideal customers are out there just waiting to be served by you.

At SarahsBookBonus.com you can find more examples of subscription box owners who have happy, loyal subscribers and thriving subscription box businesses because they niched down and serve a specific audience. Some of those examples include:

- Jamie Shahan's CRNA Swag for certified registered nurse anesthetists
- Nicole Jenney's GPig Box for guinea pig lovers and their pets
- Lisa Breitenfeldt's Cache Crate for geocachers
- Jenny Lee Hines's Flower Momma Box for busy moms who forget to celebrate themselves
- Christina Benton's Just Pizzelles for people who love pizzelles (a specific kind of Italian cookie)
- Rachel Duguay's MicroPuzzles for fans of miniature jigsaw puzzles

Action Steps

1. What are the demographics of your ideal customer? Age? Gender? Profession?

2. What are the psychographics of your ideal customer? Feelings? Struggles? Desires?

3. Why have you chosen this customer? What makes you so passionate about serving them?

4. Where do you think they hang out online or in person? Where can you go to learn more about them?

5. Why do you think they'd sign up for a subscription box? What are they hoping to gain?

Chapter 3

BUILD AN AUDIENCE

At the start of 2020, Britney Brown had a successful photography business. But because of the pandemic, by March the entire photography industry had shut down. Britney, like so many of us, found herself at home trying to figure out how to protect and support her family. And truthfully, she wasn't dealing with it well at all. She had always counted on structure and routine to manage her days and stay on track. Suddenly, all that structure and routine had disappeared. Britney's successful business had shut down overnight. Her military husband was working from home and needed the house quiet, at least occasionally—a nearly impossible task while sharing space with Britney and their five neurodivergent kids, all of whom were under 11 years old.

Because of her children, years ago Britney started down the path to her own attention-deficit/hyperactivity disorder (ADHD) diagnosis. Like any mom would, when her kids were diagnosed with ADHD, she began doing research. The descriptions she found about what was going on in her children's brains and what that meant for their daily lives sounded a lot like what Britney had been dealing with since she was a child too. This led her to see a psychologist, get tested, and seek support. As she dug further, she discovered an entire community of women just like her. Women who, as children, dealt with the same struggles. But because ADHD doesn't typically manifest the same in girls as it does in boys, they hadn't been diagnosed. Often young girls appear withdrawn or daydream and appear in their own worlds, opposed to the typically hyper and overactive behavior we usually associate with ADHD. Many of these women developed their own coping strategies based around the same kind of structure and routine that had kept Britney's life on track so far.

Now with no work and faced with the daily challenges of keeping five kids safe, healthy, and educated, Britney turned to TikTok to chronicle her experience of being a woman struggling with ADHD, especially in these unstructured times. She discovered that she was not alone. Her feed was not carefully curated or filtered in any way. Britney shared her struggles and the things that helped her get through. She was funny and interesting and, most important, she was real. She created a place for people to come and not feel alone. By showing her "mess," she helped other people feel okay about their messes. It was through this authenticity and humor that she built a following on TikTok. Her audience grew . . . and grew.

Britney is someone who looks for solutions. She sees possibilities everywhere, even and especially during times of uncertainty and chaos. Those early, messy pandemic days made her decide that she needed to start using a planner to help create some of the structure that was hard to come by now. But the ADHD brain is special, and she couldn't find a planner that worked for her, so she created one that did. She found she needed a journal that helped her prioritize tasks and build structure into her day—which was a real struggle for her. The uniqueness of her planner was that it centered on list-making. Britney leaned in to her design background and graphic-design skills. She also did a lot of research into brain science, researching what works and what doesn't work for ADHD humans, especially when it comes to design and planning. She created a planner that is based on guided list building using icons and prompts.

The planner worked well for Britney and her life, so she decided to share it with her audience. She wanted to offer it as a digital product, but the feedback from her community told her they wanted it in physical form. Britney listened, created the physical planner, and sold over 1,000 in the first week. With her planner sales booming, Britney got the idea for her Brainfetti subscription box. She wondered how her audience would feel about receiving a box of products that highlighted and celebrated the fact that "you're not the only one struggling." Once again, she turned to her followers and asked them if they would like to receive a big box of sparkly, dopamine-inducing fun items specially chosen for ADHD millennial women just like them. The response was enthusiastic to say the least. Britney launched her subscription box and sold out. She increased the number of available boxes almost immediately and sold those too. The second time she launched, she passed the 1,000-subscriber mark, and she's still growing today.

BUILD AN AUDIENCE FIRST, BUILD YOUR BUSINESS SECOND

The secret to Britney's astonishing success is simple: she built an audience of her ideal customers first, then she built and launched her products. She carefully and intentionally built a community to let people know they are not the only ones facing these challenges. She understood her ideal customer (because she is them) and then she went and found more of them. Britney built an amazing audience on TikTok before she ever thought about starting a subscription box. They were engaged, felt connected, and were invested in her—and her success. Her audience and her dedication to including them in her business resulted in an incredibly successful launch and growth that hasn't stopped yet. The same was true for Amanda (the other planner user) in Chapter 2, and it was true for me when I first began my subscription box business.

When I launched my box, my gift shop had already been in business for a few years. I had been posting on social media in different ways, and at least a small audience of people were paying attention to me. Specifically, people who already identified with me and liked my products. Additionally, in order to take my subscription box business to the next level when I plateaued after a couple months, I had to once again build an audience, this time outside my local area. I had to become visible, engaging and connecting with people online. And now we all know how I had to persevere through my live-video struggles.

I see many new subscription box hopefuls fall into the trap of believing that if they create an amazing subscription box, the subscribers will simply come. They mimic the *Field of Dreams* strategy that "if they build it, they will come." They hope that people will just show up and buy. But here's the major flaw in this plan: if no one knows about what you've built, they can't buy it.

This is why I spend so much time talking to subscription box owners about audience building. After you've identified your ideal customer, it's the next step in starting, launching, and growing a subscription box. And if you want your subscription box to succeed, the audience building never stops. Subscription box hopefuls often get distracted by the fun parts of starting a subscription box. It's fun to design logos and custom boxes or to spend hours on wholesale sites researching possible products. At least that's what most of my students and I find fun. The time and effort necessary to consistently post good content on social media feels a lot more like work and a lot less like fun. Sometimes I have to seriously convince my students that this is worth their time. Building an audience sounds like a daunting task, and the thought of creating something from scratch can be intimidating. But I have some good news: this doesn't have to be that hard, and in the end, you might even actually find it fun.

START WITH THE AUDIENCE YOU HAVE

We'll get into the nitty-gritty practical tips about how and when to post on social media in a few pages. But I want to start with this truth: you already have an audience. Even if you don't think you have one, you do. Any subscription box hopeful naturally builds an audience before they even have a business. Think about it. You have a network; you know people. Almost certainly, if you have interests, you've shared them with others. Likely you have social media accounts, and if you're truly passionate about your subscription box idea, you might have even begun posting about it in some fashion. In the beginning, who is going to buy from you? It's who you already know, these people who are already in your network. Your friends start to buy from you; your family members start to buy from you. Then they tell someone in their network about you or show a friend or neighbor something that they bought from you. It sets off this little chain reaction of people who start to follow you or buy something from you. Our whole lives, we're essentially audience building, even though you haven't been thinking about it in those terms.

It starts with the people we meet along the way. It's the convention that you go to, the moms' day out you attend every other Thursday, or the people you volunteer with each month. Those little things you do in your everyday life start building your audience, and you simply need to continue to do them as you build your business. Online, it's the networking channels that you add yourself to, the courses you take, the memberships you've joined, and the groups on Facebook you're a part of. If you look at it as just socializing and being around people that are like you, you don't see it as intentionally building an audience. It feels natural, something you automatically do as a human being. You're simply networking, making friends, sharing your passion.

Eventually, the first time will come around when someone you don't know follows you or comments on a post. I remember this feeling—it's incredible. You finally feel legit because it's not just your mom or your sister or your next-door neighbor paying attention. That said, do not be ashamed of those early followers (or customers!) and small beginnings. Everyone starts at the same place, and those first audience members are a gigantic win, no matter who they are. Just know that eventually you will grow. You will find people who don't know you. Soon it's not just your best friend who supports you and listens to you talk about your business over margaritas. The first time someone you don't know engages with your content online and eventually wants to buy what you're selling, it's enormously validating. Lean in to that. Ask yourself who this person is.

What are they like? Where do they hang out? Where do I find more people just like them for my business? That's when the real audience building begins.

People think audience building is hard because they think they don't know what to do. But, spoiler alert: YOU DO. You've already been doing it. You just have to keep focusing on your ideal customer and figure out where they spend their time, both in person and online. Then simply do what you've done to build a network your entire life. Go and hang out in more of the places your ideal customer hangs out, and network with those people. Be genuine, serve them, and provide value. That's how to do it without feeling slimy or salesy. The first step is to place yourself in situations where you'll be where your people are.

YOUR AUDIENCE-BUILDING STRATEGY

All right, so now you know who your ideal customer is and that you need to find more of them to build an audience before you launch your box. So, let's get down to the strategies to make it happen.

90 Days

If you are completely starting from scratch, meaning you don't have an audience or an existing business yet, I recommend spending at least 90 days building an audience, finding the people who will be interested in your box. Don't worry about selling anything right now. We're not there yet, and I'll coach you through it when we do get there. Instead, you're just gathering like-minded people who have a similar interest and planting seeds. If you do have an existing business or audience, you might not need to build an audience at all and could probably launch your subscription box business in as little as 30 days if you wanted. Some of my students highlighted in this book added a subscription box business to create a new revenue stream using an audience they already had.

As you know from the Introduction, even though I had an existing business, I still spent 90 days prepping and planning. Before I launched my subscription box, I started asking my customers what they thought about the idea. They responded enthusiastically, giving me incredibly valuable feedback. I built on my customers' excitement, engaging them in polls that I used for my research. They felt involved in the process, which increased their excitement for what was coming even more. I talked about my future subscription box every week, to keep it top of mind for them. So, if you're feeling brave and excited enough, go ahead and tell people you're doing this! That's the best form of accountability. When you put it out there and know other people are watching and expecting it, you're much more likely to follow through. You can add a "coming soon" banner on your social media pages and start teasing what you're doing.

If you don't want to begin with announcing that you're starting a subscription box, that's totally fine. Eventually, you will have to. The most important thing is to begin establishing a connection with your ideal customer. Social media allows us to reach people in a way we've never been able to, and people crave connection. People want to be part of something. They want to connect with the brands they buy from and the people behind those brands. Social media provides a way for you to build a personal connection with your audience, even if you never meet them in real life.

People want to be part of something. They want to connect with the brands they buy from and the people behind those brands.

Before we discuss what and how often to post, remember that all followers are not good followers. Don't fall prey to the vanity numbers trap. Some entrepreneurs concentrate their efforts on attracting followers simply to boost their numbers. But 5,000 of the right followers have much more value than 25,000 of the wrong followers. Your goal is to attract your right followers—those people who are your ideal customers.

If you're just getting started with audience building, I recommend starting with one platform and layering in more as you get consistent. Choose the platform where your ideal customer is most likely to hang out, or perhaps which one you just like the best. Social media and the landscape online are constantly changing, so we won't get into the differences between Instagram and Facebook. Instead, we'll cover timeless principles you can apply to any form of media to build your audience.

Once you've chosen your platform, it's time to create a plan to post consistently. Again, it's important to post, even though you are not yet selling products. Focus on creating shareable content. What I mean by that is content that is so relatable to the reader that they feel compelled to share it on their own social media. It's speaking to your ideal customer in a way that only they would understand. Think about a time where you saw a post and it was so spot on you just had to share it. It could be funny, it could be a life hack, it could be educational, but it's so good, you want to share it with other people who are just like you. Which ultimately attracts more of the same person: your ideal customer. The goal is to increase your reach, to get in front of people who do not yet know about you or your brand. Every time someone shares one of your posts, you are getting in front of more people. And if the person sharing your content is your ideal customer, chances are high that some of their friends or followers are too.

Here are some ideas of what to post:

- Memes that speak directly to your ideal customer
- How-tos explaining something helpful
- Life hacks
- Inspirational posts—quotes, pictures, interesting thoughts
- Engagement posts—polls, asking questions to receive feedback
- Behind-the-scenes posts—what products you're considering, what you're doing that day, progress on your box

Only after you've launched:

- Customer and subscriber reviews as social proof
- Products themselves

When you're truly stuck about what to post, don't over-complicate it. Think about your own social media use. What stops your scroll? What do you like and click on? Why do you think that is? You can even look at other brands and see what they're posting if you need some inspiration. If your ideal client is you, whatever you're liking and clicking on will resonate with them as well. Remember, this doesn't have to be hard. Just think about the lifestyle and behaviors of your ideal customers.

Once you have a couple weeks of posts under your belt, do a little analysis. What seems to get the most attention (likes, shares, comments, and so on)? Then your one simple plan is to Do. More. Of. That. If nothing sticks out quite yet, that's okay, keep experimenting. Find what works and keep doing it.

I also look at the posts themselves. Your posts need to grab someone's attention. That means images that catch their eye and posts that don't have too much text. You can create great posts quickly and easily using Canva, a graphic-design platform that allows someone to create designs for social media, presentations, and so many other things. It provides templates, images, and different customizable design elements. It's user friendly and one of my favorite tools. You can also just use product photos you've taken with your phone.

Posting Schedule

The most important element in the timing of your posting is that you are consistent. Do not post three times one day and then not again for a week. Social media, your followers, and the algorithm don't respond well to that. It's a much better strategy to be reliable and predictable so they see you regularly and you stick in their minds. Start with one post per day, and work up to three posts per day if you can. Here is my exact daily social media strategy that I've followed for years now:

Sarah's Social Media Strategy

I post two to three times a day every day:

- One engagement post
- One product post, including subscriptions
- One free post, usually a product post, but can be anything I want to post about

Let's Talk about Video

Your goal on social media is to stop the scroll. People's attention spans continue to get shorter, which means you need to capture them quickly. Live videos are a great way to accomplish this. If you want to increase your reach, connect with your audience, and create raving fans, live video needs to be part of your marketing strategy. Of course, I know the idea of going live might terrify you. It terrified me, remember? In Chapter 1, I shared my struggle with showing up and accepting my role as the influencer for my business. Those old feelings of self-doubt stood in my way, even after I realized what I needed to do and even had a little experience.

But my desire to succeed and grow my subscription box business was bigger than my fear. And so I showed up, posted on social media consistently, and went live on video every Friday morning to engage with my audience in real time. That audience grew, and you can still find me there every week, sharing new products with them and making sales. If I hadn't done the work to find and build an audience outside of my local area, my subscription box business would not have grown to where it is today— thousands of monthly subscribers strong. The truth is, you will build your audience faster, connect with that audience more deeply, and likewise allow them to connect to you by being with them on live video. There is no quicker way to build a personal relationship with your audience and attract your ideal customer. Plus the immediate feedback you'll receive about your ideas and products is invaluable. You can just ask them right there what they want from you, what their struggles are, and how you can help them.

The Five Parts of (Live) Video

Something that helped me early on in my journey to live-video confidence just might help you too. I used it back when the thought of going live made me sweaty and nauseous, and I still use it today. My mentor, Stu McLaren, who you heard from in the Foreword to this book, teaches the following framework:

1. A hook. This is what catches your audience's attention. Think of it like a newspaper headline.

2. A story. Tell a personal story or talk about the inspiration behind your box or whatever you're about to show/teach them.

3. Teaching points. For product-based businesses, these are the actual products. Show them the goods! It could also be how to use a particular product.

4. Your call to action. Tell them what to do next. Sign up for the waitlist, go to your online shop, and so on.

5. A recap. Quickly review the top four points before you end the video.

    Here's an example of how this might look:

1. Your cashmere scarf isn't just for winter anymore! (Hook)

2. A story of when you wore your pashmina scarf in the summer, and it was great. (Story)

3. Three ways to wear your scarf with cute summer outfits. (Teaching points)

    a. Outfit one

    b. Outfit two

    c. Outfit three

4. If you like this scarf, sign up for my subscription box! I send out items exactly like this. (Call to action)

5. Here are the three ways to wear the scarf in summer and how to get one of your own. (Recap)

If you feel worried or uncomfortable about live video, use this framework to write out notes. You'll feel more prepared and able to settle in and enjoy your time with your audience, which of course will help build a connection. One day every week, I go live on the two platforms I use, and I'm incredibly consistent. I show up at the same time every week, and my audience shows up for me too. For someone who almost didn't push the damn button, I've come a long way. You will too.

Let's break for a little pep talk. You may avoid doing live videos because you worry you'll embarrass yourself or that you are not interesting enough. Trust me, you are interesting enough. You have a passion for what you do and a passion for serving your audience. Trust that your passion will come through and your audience will connect with you because of it. As for embarrassing moments, they'll happen. They'll also serve to make you relatable to your audience. They'll like you more for it. I've certainly embarrassed myself more than a few times during live videos! To help you be brave and confident during live video, here are some strategies you can implement:

1. Do something for yourself that makes you feel confident. Get a new outfit, style your hair, strike a power pose—whatever helps you get in front of the camera.

2. Ask a few friends to join your live video and give them questions to ask you to get the conversation going.

3. Write out your talking points to help with nerves and to make sure you cover what you want to talk about.

4. Engage with your audience. Whether one person shows up or 100, they want to make a personal connection with you. Keep up with the comments and have a conversation.

5. Set a consistent day and time for your live videos and send it out so you'll stick to it. Make it a time that works for you.

The truth is in the numbers. If you don't incorporate live video into your audience-building strategy and create a personal relationship with your audience, you'll find growing your subscriber base to be slow and difficult. When I conquered my fears of going live, I saw an immediate difference. I was finally able to break through the plateau I had been stuck at with my subscription box. I promise this is a worthwhile strategy.

Start Your E-mail List

Social media and live video are extremely important, but they're not the end of our audience-building strategy. The main goal of all this content creation, other than making sales, is to build an e-mail list. It's important to realize you don't own your social media accounts. Those platforms actually own your accounts. Social media sites go down, and accounts get hacked or frozen all the time. Imagine if you have thousands of followers and your account gets hacked. In an instant you lose access to all those people you worked so hard to connect with. Would you have any way to get in touch with them? You cannot place all your eggs in the social media basket. It's like building your business on rental property—you could get kicked out at any moment. What you need is something you own, a way to get in touch with your audience no matter what. You need a way to stay connected with them, sell them products, and add value that doesn't depend on these social media platforms always being around. That's what your e-mail list is for.

An active, growing e-mail list is an incredibly valuable asset to your business. E-mail and social media are not an either-or situation. You need both in order to build your audience and successfully launch and grow your subscription box. My e-mail list is hard at work every day for my business. Thirty percent of all of my sales come from e-mail, and when I get subscriber cancellations, they're filled instantly by sending one e-mail to my waitlist. These days, there are countless easy-to-use platforms to begin building your e-mail list. Many of them you can even sign up to start for free. Here are the basics. You need two things in order to start building your list:

1. An e-mail platform (or CRM, customer relationship manager, as they say in the biz) (See some of my top up-to-date suggestions at SarahsBookBonus.com)

2. Website/landing page for people to sign up (Some e-mail systems even have mechanisms to allow you to create and host a landing page directly on their platform. This is a great option if you haven't built your website yet.)

An e-mail CRM is your e-mail marketing software. This is not the same as Gmail, Yahoo mail, or other personal e-mail providers. A CRM allows you to do so much more than just send e-mails. There are great CRMs designed specifically for e-commerce that serve the needs of subscription box owners incredibly well (see my preferred resources at SarahsBookBonus.com). They're usually intuitive and easy to set up and manage. Klaviyo is one I always recommend inside my membership and use for my own e-commerce site. It places a strong emphasis on data-driven, personalized e-mail campaigns and has a number of features specifically geared toward e-commerce businesses (like built-in abandoned cart recovery e-mail flows and the ability to trigger post-purchase follow-up e-mails based on customer behaviors).

4 Ways to Grow Your E-mail List

1. **Ask people to join.** This one is clear enough, right? Just plain ask people to join. Let them know this is how to best stay in touch with you and hear about when the box launches, special discounts, offers, fun content, and so on. You don't even have to know exactly what to e-mail yet. Just tell people you are starting one, and start one.

2. **Run a giveaway.** A giveaway is a great way to generate interest in your subscription box before you even have one. I suggest running giveaways two to four times a year even after your subscription box is well-established. They are still part of my ongoing audience-building efforts. Make sure to pick a winning prize that would naturally appeal to your ideal customer and might even be something you would put in a box someday. You could also offer your exact subscription box as a one-time gift. I just did this for my T-Shirt subscription box and offered it especially for teachers. The gift was a six-month free subscription to the box for themselves and their teacher bestie, because most teachers have tons of friends who are also teachers. People naturally shared this with all of their teacher friends. It created a lot of buzz and was so much fun. It added 1,300 new e-mail addresses to my list and many more social media subscribers, and the cost to me was minimal. There are several giveaway apps and plugins that make running an online giveaway easy. My favorite is KingSumo, which can quickly create a landing page for your giveaway and customize the look and feel to match your brand. (See more at SarahsBookBonus.com.)

3. Create a lead magnet that people receive when they sign up. These can be e-books, checklists, tutorials, discount codes, or free downloads like wallpaper or printable art. Anything to incentivize people to sign up. Again, keep your ideal customer in mind. What do you think they'd appreciate from you? What do you like receiving from companies? One of my favorite things to do is create a resource that answers a lot of questions that your audience has. (You know what those questions are because you know your ideal customer and have been so engaged with them on social media already, right?) Here are a few more ideas:

- Recipes
- Supply lists
- Cheat sheets
- Transcripts of podcast episodes/videos
- Worksheets
- Patterns or templates

4. Create a pop-up or flyout on your website. I know, I know. Pop-ups get a bad rap and can be annoying. But the reason they still exist is because they work! You can use these to remind people to sign up for your e-mail list.

The Money Is in the (Wait)List

As soon as you start your e-mail list, start a waitlist for your subscription box. This is an e-mail list specifically for people who are interested in knowing about your subscription box when you launch. If you're just starting your business, the waitlist for your subscription box may be the only e-mail list you have, which is perfectly fine. If you haven't already, let your audience know it's coming. Tell them why it's important for them to join. They want to be the first ones signed up to make sure they don't miss out. Every time you talk about your coming subscription box, your call to action is to sign up for the waitlist. The people on your waitlist will be your hottest buyers. This list will also determine your goal number of subscribers for your first box. So if you want a big first month, hype that e-mail list.

As soon as you have an e-mail list, begin e-mailing them once a week. Yes, that's right. E-mail them once a week, every week, all year, even if you don't have your box up and running yet. *But Sarah, what should I e-mail to my list? I don't have anything to sell them yet.* I know, and that's completely fine. That's the point even. Don't overcomplicate this. Share the exact kinds of things you're already sharing on social media. Repurpose that content and send it to your e-mail list. Share links to the videos you've made, posts that did well on social, helpful content you created. You can even just update your subscribers on how the box is coming along and share sneak peeks of what will be in them. The important thing is that you stay in touch with your list and keep connecting with the people on it. This is a chance for you to show them that you're exactly like them, care for them, and that your box is worth the subscription.

A SUCCESSFUL LAUNCH STARTS WITH AUDIENCE BUILDING

The hard truth is that if you don't spend the time building an audience, they won't come. If you don't create awareness, attract your ideal customer, and show them what you are offering and its value to them, they won't show up. In fact, when someone in my membership, Launch Your Box, posts about having a disappointing launch, I jump into problem-solving mode, and I start with examining their audience-building efforts. Their social media accounts give me an instant picture of what they have and haven't been doing.

A subscription box owner may say, "Sarah, I did everything you taught, everything I was supposed to do, and it just didn't work." Nine times out of ten, with some investigating, I discover they're not getting results because of the reasons that follow.

3 Reasons Why Launches Fail

Before we wrap up this chapter, I want to explain to you the top three reasons why I see subscription box launches fail. *But, Sarah, why are we talking about launching now? I've barely even started growing my audience?!* Because, sister, the success of your launches starts here:

1. **Inconsistent social media presence.** Maybe they posted one day last week, three times another week, three times in one day a while ago, and then ghosted their social media for the last five days. Social media platforms don't respond well to sporadic posting and neither do audiences. One more time for the people in the back: post consistently.

2. **Their messaging is confusing, and they're not speaking to a specific person.** It's so important to know who your ideal customer is; to understand what that person is thinking, doing, and feeling; and to talk to them in their language. Your messaging needs to speak to this person. If you try to speak to everyone, you won't attract anyone. Don't speak to people who love hiking in the Northwest one day and Southern moms with minivans the next. Talk to your person (i.e., you!).

3. **Their engagement is low.** If someone has a low number of followers but they're engaged, that's a good sign. They just need to keep doing what they're doing, and their followers will grow. However, a high number of followers with low engagement is a problem. A large number of followers does no good if they're not engaging with you. Unengaged followers don't turn into subscribers. You could have followers not engaging for a number of reasons:

   - **Poor content quality.** Can you make your content more interesting, relevant, or valuable to your audience?

   - **Lack of connection.** Are you actively building a relationship with your audience?

   - **Competition.** Does your content stand out from the crowd?

By the time I wrap up my detective work, the reasons for the less-than-stellar launch are usually very clear, and it almost always doesn't have anything to do with the products they chose or anything that happened during launch week. It's about this all-important foundational work that we're covering here.

It is so important to serve before selling. This takes time and consistency.

Starting a subscription box business is hard (but fun!) work. It's incredibly rewarding, and the recurring revenue it brings can be life-changing. But you have to do the work. You have to take the steps to get ready and give yourself the best chance at success. Building an audience of your ideal customers is crucial. Find them and make it easy for them to find you. You can launch a box without an audience to launch it to, but it won't be successful. Audience building means finding those people who your box is right for and inviting them into your world. Then you need to engage them, provide them with value, and build connections. It is so important to serve before selling. This takes time and consistency. It takes showing up for your people—and then showing up over and over again. Yes, you want to do everything you can to rapidly build your audience in the next 90 days. But think of audience building as a long-term goal, and make it a priority every day. It is not something to check off your to-do list and forget about. In order to build a successful subscription box business, you need to commit to constantly working at it. Building an audience takes consistency and dedication. It takes a willingness to engage and connect with people, sharing yourself and your business with them. Remember, you don't need a huge audience—you just need the right one.

Action Steps

1. Decide on just one social media platform to begin. Which one will you choose to focus your efforts on?

2. Set a launch date. Give yourself 90 days to build your audience.

3. Create a posting schedule. Find some helpful worksheets for this at SarahsBookBonus.com. Commit to posting once a day at first and work up to three times a day.

4. Do a live video. Just go for it! Plan it out, schedule it, tell people you're doing it, and hit the button. Make it short and sweet at first. And enlist some buddies to show up and ask questions and support you.

5. Run a giveaway.

6. Decide on an e-mail CRM, and officially start your e-mail list.

7. Announce to your audience that you're starting a subscription box, and start a waitlist.

Chapter 4

CULTIVATE COMMUNITY

Jenny Lee Hines is the founder of the Flower Momma Box, a subscription box dedicated to celebrating busy moms who don't take the time, or have the time, to celebrate life's big and little wins. I love Jenny's mission and what has come out of her initial idea to shine a light on the behind-the-scenes busyness that is so much a part of the lives of moms of young children.

The Flower Momma Box is actually Jenny's rebranded subscription box, her version 2.0. Version 1.0 was also a flower box, but it wasn't growing the way Jenny had hoped. Her product was solid—gorgeous flowers arranged artfully into bouquets any woman would be thrilled to receive. She was posting on social media and e-mailing her list the way I'd coached her to. So when she started losing subscribers, she was confused and knew she needed more help. When she sent me a discouraged message, I immediately hopped on the phone with her to troubleshoot what might be holding her back.

Part of the issue was something we discussed in Chapter 2. Jenny hadn't niched down far enough. So instead of just focusing on all moms, she decided to narrow her focus to moms of young children and address the specific stress, exhaustion, loneliness, and beauty that comes with that particular time in motherhood. But that wasn't the only change she made to course correct her business. Jenny is a people person—a giver, a talker, a feeler, and a strong Christian. I knew and loved this about her, and I knew her customers would too, because likely they were similar. What she needed to do was not only have a great product, social content, and e-mail list but also create a community.

WE ALL WANT TO BELONG

We all want to feel as if we belong. As social beings, we crave community. That's why we join clubs, organizations, and networking groups. Coming together around a common interest or cause makes us feel connected. Plus it's just fun! When you create community among your subscribers, you give them a sense of belonging to something, a shared experience. Subscribers who feel connected in this way are more likely to be loyal to you and your brand. Those are the customers who become more than just repeat customers—they become brand ambassadors or even raving fans. Kevin Kelly wrote an article in 2008 that is well-known and quoted in the entrepreneurial community called "1,000 True Fans." (An updated version appears in Tim Ferriss's book *Tools of Titans*.) The gist is that 1,000 diehard fans are all you need to create a successful business. A true fan is exactly what I described earlier: someone who will buy absolutely anything you sell. They're on your waitlist for everything, preorder your products, watch your videos, like your posts, and show up for your events every time. Kelly calls them fans; I call them community.

These people will also tell their family, friends, neighbors, and co-workers (many of whom may be potential subscribers) about you and your subscription. This type of social proof marketing is invaluable to you as you build your subscription business. In other words, another pro of building a community is that it's an extremely valuable marketing asset.

Jenny and I talked about this on our call, and she began to implement some community-building techniques. Young motherhood is a topic ripe for conversation and community, so Jenny started *The Flower Momma* podcast, where she talks about challenges facing moms of young children. She also interviews others who bring clarity or shine a light on these challenges and ways to bring more positivity and celebration into the lives of Jenny's "Flower Mommas."

Being part of Jenny's community of subscribers means exclusive access to her in-person workshops. Subscribers who are not local are able to take part virtually. Each subscriber is allowed to bring along a plus-one to participate in the workshop, and those people are invited to become subscribers during the workshop. And guess what? Jenny converts nearly 100 percent of the plus-ones into subscribers. Can you think of anything more community building than that?

The last change Jenny made was including a monthly self-reflection in the Flower Momma Box, asking members to write down their "roses, blooms, and thorns" for the month and share them. Roses are the good things that happened, blooms are what they're looking forward to or planning for the next month, and the thorns are the difficult things they experienced. In addition, Jenny includes a printout of something meaningful she's written.

Jenny gets deep with her subscribers. They share personal experiences, often requesting prayers and a compassionate shoulder to lean on, and Jenny provides that. Her subscription box is so much more than a business. For her, it's a ministry dedicated to serving a group of women who spend their days serving others. As a fellow mom, I remember so well those days when my own kids were young. The days can be long, filled with fixing meals and snacks, wiping up endless crumbs (or worse!), picking up toys, and managing small people's big emotions. It's easy for moms to come to the end of the day feeling like they didn't really accomplish anything. Jenny helps these mommas realize there are reasons to celebrate every day, big and small.

What I want you to notice is that this community Jenny built doesn't actually revolve around flowers. The mommas love their flowers, but everything Jenny created—the podcast, community, and even the workshops—aren't about flowers. They're about the needs and desires of her ideal customer. Jenny has identified them (Chapter 2), gone out to find them / attracted them to her (Chapter 3), and is now creating a sense of belonging and community among them (Chapter 4). That's the point of all the social media posting and e-mail list building. Jenny cultivates conversations around where her subscribers are in their lives. She celebrates the wins and doesn't shy away from the hard times. Her subscribers know she is in their corner, willing to listen to them and always ready to pray for them. She is intentional with everything she does, striving to make every contact with her audience deeper and more meaningful. That is how you build a community. And that is how you build a successful business.

Selling your boxes is important. I mean, hey, it's the reason you're here, right? You want a successful subscription box business. You want to make money. So do I. But in this journey, never forget that each of your subscribers is a person who matters. They're not just a number on your e-mail list or a thumbs-up on a social media post. They're a person who is looking for connection. And if you offer it to them, they'll stick with you forever. Now let's get into some ways to do that.

> *Never forget that each of your subscribers is a person who matters.*

5 WAYS TO CULTIVATE COMMUNITY WITH YOUR IDEAL CUSTOMERS

Cultivating a community can benefit a product-based business in several ways. Loyal customers who are invested in your success and feel a part of something are far more likely to make repeat purchases, offer word-of-mouth referrals, and give you valuable feedback about your products. This feeling of community builds that all-important know, like, and trust factor that is critical in business and creates buy-in on the customer's end. And most essentially, it creates a sense of belonging. You have built community in your personal life; creating it in business is not so different.

1. Live Video

You've heard me talk about live video a few times already in this book, and there is more to come. (So if you thought you were off the live-video hook, think again. You can do it!) The reason live video works so well, besides all the social media algorithms that constantly change, is that it is the most meaningful way to connect with people other than being in person. It was the mechanism for me being able to reach subscribers outside of my hometown because it was the next best thing to people walking into my shop. And it's a way for subscribers to connect with each other. One of the reasons having a small audience is a benefit at the beginning is because your subscribers can get to know each other. If it's the same few people every time popping onto your video, they'll recognize the names and can chat in the comments. Remember, some great ideas for live video include showcasing ways to use products, box reveals (after you've launched), and tutorials. For more ways to utilize live video, refer to Chapter 3.

2. Texting

Yes, you can actually text with your customers. Since it's coming directly to your phone, it feels much more personal than an e-mail or a post in a group. Don't worry; you don't have to give out your real phone number to strangers, no matter how lovely they are. There are plenty of texting apps these days that mask your real number and allow you to chat with subscribers. Just do a quick search, and you'll find a few good ones.

My subscribers love to receive texts from me and they're great at replying. I ask them to share their favorite item from that month's box or a picture of them using a product. Then I share these pics on my social media with a cute little graphic including their name, which makes them feel like a valued member of the community and provides great social proof. (Tip: always get their permission before posting.) Jenny also uses her texting app to communicate with her subscribers regularly, checking in with them throughout the month and asking them how she can pray for them. This is a crucial way she creates personal connections with those subscribers who need support from her.

3. Social Media Groups

We all know about this one, right? If you're anything like me, you've been a part of different social media groups since Facebook had fan groups of different bands. Groups on different social media platforms still remain a great way to bring people together. It's also one of the simplest ways to start building a community. Groups also allow you to implement a certain measure of privacy, where group members know that what they share is not being seen by everyone in the social media universe but only by other group members, which may help them feel less vulnerable about honestly sharing their thoughts, feelings, or experiences.

4. Events

Jenny utilized this one too with her bouquet-assembling workshops. Any kind of event that brings people together and creates conversation around a shared interest is a great way to foster community. If you can do this in person, that's fantastic.

I host Subscriber Pick-Up parties for my local audience. And a few times a year we do a big warehouse sale for those same people, complete with giveaways and food trucks in the parking lot. Subscribers can come and not only pick up their boxes but shop the sale, grab a bite to eat, meet the warehouse team, and take pictures with our logo backdrop.

Kasey Hope, owner of Whatever Letter and a Launch Your Box member, has a subscription box where she sends supplies every month to teach her students lettering. A few times a year she hosts a meetup in her studio in Alabama. Subscribers drive or fly in from all over to attend her events. Her main goal is community building, though these events also have the added benefit of providing great video and testimonials Kasey can use for her website and social media. Kasey mentioned that many longtime subscribers come who haven't even completed a project yet. They come to gain confidence and create something with help so they can go home and do it on their own.

But you don't have to only orchestrate in-person events. There are some great ways to do this virtually as well. On social media, within groups, or on a hosting platform like Zoom, you can create a virtual meetup. Here are some ideas for events:

- Invite a guest speaker to share about a topic your audience is interested in.
- Teach something (like Jenny).
- Host a party, for any reason!
- Have subscribers come on and share their experiences.

5. Podcasts or Shows

I have a podcast called *Launch Your Box,* and it's one of the main ways I'm able to connect with my current audience and find new subscription box hopefuls. Although you aren't interacting in real time, podcasts are a great way to get right in the eardrums of your ideal customers and connect with them. Another version of this is creating a regular "show" on YouTube or a social media platform. Jess Connolly did this for a while with something called the *Made Up Morning Show* on Instagram where she went live and talked about what she had planned for the day, things on her mind, and gave a little dose of inspiration and motivation.

The members of my Launch Your Box membership get creative when it comes to building community with and for their subscribers. Of course, I hope you steal some of the strategies I described earlier, but I also hope you're inspired to brainstorm new and creative ways you can make your subscribers feel like valued members of your world. There are endless ways to create community for your ideal customers, and they all start with creating a connection between you and them.

HAVE SOME FUN

Jenny created a deep, thoughtful, and intimate community among her subscribers. But your version of community can be different. You don't have to share all the details of your life if you don't want to. Sometimes a beautiful community can emerge just from the desire to have fun. My student

Stacey Collins did that. Every month, thousands of women wait for a delivery from Stacey. Unlike the women who stalk their porches waiting for my turquoise boxes, these women sit at their computers hitting the refresh button. They're not waiting for their subscription to be delivered to their front porches; this one comes to their e-mail inboxes.

Stacey first built her blog around revamping Dollar Tree crafts. She would go to her local Dollar Tree, buy a craft or some cheap supplies, and improve upon them to create something beautiful. Her audience loved it. Everyone has a local dollar store, and Stacey made every project seem so doable. Her style is gorgeous and classic; it was hard to believe that she created these crafts from cheap material. She describes herself as a lover of all things decorating, crafting, and shopping. She created videos, social media posts, and tutorials all teaching her followers to do exactly what she does. Her philosophy is that you can have a beautifully decorated home without spending a lot of money. She empowered her audience to create cute, display-worthy crafts to use as part of those decorations. Stacey brings a sense of fun and excitement to everything she does, including her "whisper shopping" trips on her social media page, where she shares fun finds and great deals and she quietly talks to the camera while she shops. I love watching these videos, and so do her more than 200,000 followers.

In 2020, Stacey started going live on social media a lot, crafting and just hanging out with her audience. Her followers, like many of us during that time, were spending more time at home than ever before. They craved connection and found comfort in creating together. These ladies were looking for a way to craft at home on a budget and have fun with online friends while they did it. Stacey provided that for them with her own special brand of personality and creativity.

The demand to think of new ideas for more crafts to work on with her audience was high, so Stacey introduced the idea of crafting with printables—designs she created that people could print out and put in a frame or use as a starting point for a craft. They're quicker, cheaper, and easier to access than most traditional crafts, plus she was already creating them for herself. She created printables occasionally for her blog, so she began to experiment. Each month, Stacey's subscribers received an e-mail with a link to the exclusive printables she designed for them. They use these printables for crafting projects and home-decor items.

Stacey's audience loved the printable craft and asked her to create more. She started selling them in her online store, and they sold very well. And there was a group of customers who bought every printable Stacey created—her true, raving fans. Without realizing it, they basically asked for a subscription. That's how the Printable Club—a digital subscription for crafters and DIYers—began. As someone who focuses on serving her audience, Stacey realized a monthly subscription would allow her most loyal printable customers to receive all of her designs and save a lot of money doing it.

The first launch of the Printable Club resulted in 800 subscribers. Stacey already had a sizable engaged audience who she had worked hard to create relationships with. They knew, liked, and trusted her. She listened to them and gave them what they wanted. Within two years, the Printable Club grew to more than 2,000 subscribers, which meant Stacey had more than $30,000 of recurring revenue coming in every month.

Every month, Stacey goes live on social media to reveal that month's exclusive designs. She also asks her subscribers to share pictures of projects they complete with their printables so others in the community can see them and gain inspiration. This allows them to show off their creativity and encourage and support one another. Friendships are formed, as crafters love to talk shop with each other. By encouraging this sharing on the page and interacting with her subscribers there, Stacey generates excitement (and more than a little FOMO—fear of missing out) among audience members who aren't yet subscribers. Subscribers regularly text Stacey and tag her in social media posts, sharing their excitement about the Printable Club and the projects they are able to create with her printables. The feedback is incredibly valuable, as Stacey listens carefully when they tell her what they want more of and takes advantage of every opportunity to show love and appreciation for her many loyal subscribers. The continued success of the Printable Club has much to do with Stacey's laser focus on community.

Her customers don't just feel connected to Stacey, they also feel connected to each other, all without creating a formal, private social media community. Stacey's community is built around crafting and fun. It's not as deep and personal as Jenny's, although it's no less meaningful. The success of Stacey's digital subscription shows just how powerful a connected community can be. When you serve sincerely, listen to your audience, and meet them where they are and where they want to be, there's no limit to where you can take your business.

Subscription box owners create community in many different ways, but the feeling is the same. Think about the time, money, and effort you place into gaining a new follower, getting them onto your waitlist, and finally converting them into a subscriber. Don't forget to invest just as much time and energy into building a community they'll want to be a part of for a very long time. This is the difference between having a subscription box people are interested in for a couple months and then cancel and having a thriving business for years to come. Create something others want to be a part of, find your true fans and community, and you'll never be wanting for customers.

Action Steps

1. Brainstorm the kind of community you want to create around your subscription box. You can create something deep like Jenny or fun and whimsical like Stacey. Whatever you do, just do it intentionally.

2. Review the five ways to cultivate community, and pick one to implement.

Chapter 5

CREATE AN EXPERIENCE

The packages you will send out to your subscribers are about so much more than the products inside of them. Curating boxes is so much fun, and we'll delve into exactly how to do that in the next chapter. But before you pick your first physical products, you have to understand what's really going on here. When done right, a package fills your subscribers with anticipation before they even open it. Even small details add to the excitement and the pleasure of discovering what's inside. Every time you send a box to a customer, you have the opportunity to make it something to celebrate.

A few years ago, I ordered an Erin Condren planner. I'm still a paper planner person, and hers are my favorites. (Yes, the Venn diagram between subscription box lovers/ owners and people who love planners is almost just one circle.) I love everything about them, from the variety of designs to the ways I can customize them to make them my own. This particular planner was a limited edition. I was so excited when I was able to preorder it months before. Many of Erin's planners sell out, and I knew that if I didn't order it way in advance, that limited-edition planner might be gone.

Of course, preordering the planner meant I had to wait for a long time. Preorders often occur before the products are ready to ship, or sometimes before they're even finished being made. During those months, my anticipation continued to build. Every time I saw a planner out in the wild, I remembered that mine was coming soon. And every sneak peek and e-mail Erin sent out in the meantime reminded me of how great it was going to be. I just knew it was going to be fabulous. When I received the e-mail that it had been shipped, I checked that tracking status every day until it arrived. Finally, I walked up to my front porch, and there it was, just waiting for me. I couldn't resist opening it right away. The box was a beautiful blue, and every detail was perfect. The planner was wrapped in custom tissue paper held together with custom stickers.

The planner was amazing, of course, as I knew it would be. I was no stranger to Erin's products. I knew it would help me keep all the parts of my busy life organized. But in addition to the planner, the box contained little extras that added to the experience. Every item in the box, from the planner to the accessories to the packaging itself, had been chosen carefully. This wasn't something I had just picked up from Target (and no disrespect; I love Target!) that had been mass-produced by a manufacturer I don't even know and thrown into a red-and-white bag at checkout. Every detail added to an overall experience that was about so much more than simply receiving a new planner in the mail. I don't say this to be cheesy but entirely sincere—it made me feel special. Erin's planner, box, and presentation all made me feel appreciated. It was as if someone had assembled the package just for me with all those extra touches included simply to make me feel understood and cared about.

The same is true for your subscribers. You have the power to make them feel special. It's important to realize that your subscription box isn't actually about the items inside; it's about how it makes your customers feel. Yes, your subscribers signed up probably because you share interests or because they saw something they liked on your feed. But that's not why they stay. They stay because of the experience you provide. That experience lasts from before they receive each month's box until the next month's box is on the way.

IT'S MORE THAN A BOX

Here's the question I want you to think about before we head into the nuts and bolts of product curation and launching: How do you want your customers to feel? And how does everything from the packaging you choose to each of the items inside contribute to that feeling? The truth is anyone could probably find similar products elsewhere. I certainly don't have a monopoly on monograms and cute T-shirts. What they can't find is the connection to those items, because they were picked especially for them as a gift. Of course, the customers paid for them. But it's still a gift they're giving themselves. No matter how wonderful your box is (and I'm sure it is!), no one *needs* a subscription box. They just don't. There may be a few exceptions, but by and large, what we're delivering here is a *want*. But make no mistake, I don't consider that any less important, because we're still fulfilling a deep desire for people.

Your customers have busy lives, like you, probably. What that looks like depends on who your ideal customer is, and you know that because of all the audience- and community building you've done so far. My customers are busy Southern moms. I described some of their demographics and psychographics in Chapter 2, and let me elaborate here: they're tired; they're running around all day; and while being a mom is the best job in the world (and one I waited a long time for), their needs are often the last to be met. They don't do much for themselves, because they're so busy worrying about everyone else. And then . . . my subscription box arrives on their doorstep. It's a lovely box of products I handpicked because I want them to take a minute to enjoy something just for them. They deserve it.

Never forget that at the core you're making someone's day.

I've had plenty of subscribers tell me throughout the years that their box always seems to come on the day they needed it most, likely a hard day when they're feeling down. Occasionally someone will even tell me they cried when they received it because of how special they felt. This is the power of your subscription box business! Yes, it can make meaningful income and be lots of fun, but never forget that at the core you're making someone's day. Don't take that lightly. Think through this question: How do I want to make my customers feel? Happy? Certainly. But go deeper than that. I want my customers to feel known, loved, and understood. But your words are probably different from mine. Here are some examples of what my students say they want their customers to feel:

excited, calmed, curious, warm, fun, cozy, delighted. This exercise is unique to your specific box and customer and worth taking the time to get right.

HOW DO I WANT MY SUBSCRIBERS TO *feel*?

- excitement
- connection
- satisfaction
- curiosity
- belonging
- gratitude
- JOY
- surprise

THE ADVANTAGE OF A "SMALLER" BUSINESS

In the Introduction I told you about the amazing regular customers who were the inspiration for my subscription box. These regular customers became more than just people who bought what I was selling. I knew them and understood what mattered to them. I even learned about the people in their lives and knew the names of their kids. Over time, I built connections with them, and they became friends. These were the people who already loved what I sold and got excited about buying my new items and limited-edition stock. I wanted to provide them with a VIP experience. Something exclusive that I curated just for them.

When I researched the subscription box companies that were already out there, they were mostly big companies with thousands of subscribers. And they had terrible reviews. But the negative feedback wasn't about what was inside the box. It was about their experience. They complained about poor customer service, that their items were haphazardly thrown in the box, that they weren't similar at all to what was advertised, and sometimes even that they were of poor quality. They felt no one at the big company truly cared about them.

I realized right then what I could offer to subscribers that big businesses either couldn't or weren't interested in offering: I could give them an unmatched subscriber experience. I could show them they mattered to me and my business. At the beginning, I was a little discouraged that I couldn't afford as many items as these big companies because I didn't have the buying power they did. While the products do matter, I realized it wouldn't cost me much in materials or time to create the kind of experience I wanted for my subscribers. So that's exactly what I did and what I continue to do, month after month. The experience—every part of it—matters because my subscribers matter.

I could show them they mattered to me and my business.

This is one of the advantages you have of just starting out and having a small box subscription, at least at first. Depending on your waitlist and audience size, you may feel like you know those subscribers on your first box launch. They'll likely be on your waitlist, come to your live videos, comment on social media, and perhaps even e-mail you enough that you know their names and some details about them. Many things about starting out are hard (and get easier over time), but this is a positive aspect of these early days. Value those first people. Give them the VIP experience. Build that connection and treat them like the most important customers in the world. Someday, if you want, your list will be much bigger, and this may be harder to remember. Although now I have thousands of subscribers and don't know every name anymore, I still try to create the same experience of those first few subscribers a few years ago.

One afternoon a month, I go live inside Launch Your Box for member box openings. I set up my laptop camera, make sure I have coffee and water nearby, and spend about two hours opening boxes my students have sent in. I start with the outside packaging and work my way inside, talking through the experience the box provides. I give feedback and suggestions, and the members who are on with us ask questions and provide their feedback as well.

Every time, I'm amazed at the creativity of my members. But every once in a while, one of them takes the subscriber experience to a whole new level. Katie Eney is one of those members. Katie describes her subscription, the Literary Book Club Box, as "a quarterly luxury subscription box for old souls and romantics." Her box isn't just for people who read the classics. It's for people who truly love these books, who know their value. The care Katie puts into every detail makes it clear she knows her ideal customer so well. She treats her customers, and the books inside the box, with such love and respect.

I opened Katie's box to find a beautiful special-edition hardcover of *Little Women* by Louisa May Alcott. The book itself was beautiful enough to let me know this box was something special. She also provided a custom insert that guided subscribers through the experience they were going to have with this book. She included small, individually wrapped gifts to be opened as her subscribers read along. Each was labeled with a page number and any necessary instructions. They included items like a variety of tea to brew and sip while reading a particular scene, a candle to light with a scent that matched the setting on those pages, and a tiny jar of jam in the same flavor one of the characters made. I mean, come on! For a classic book lover, this is book-reading heaven.

Every item in Katie's box had a purpose. Each one worked together to create the experience her subscriber would have while reading the book. This box was about so much more than simply reading a classic book. Katie was not only offering them something they wanted but also making them feel something. The thought and care put into what she had curated was enough to make anyone feel special.

Remember, your subscribers come because they want what's inside your box. They stay because of the way your box makes them feel and the experience you provide them. That is about so much more than the items inside. It's important to realize the impact your subscription box can have on your subscribers' lives—and not take that lightly. You can turn someone's day around, guide them through a new adventure, help them discover an interest, give them a cute outfit, teach them a skill, offer them a hobby, and so on. The goal is to know your ideal customer so well that you can give them the kind of experience you know they'll love. Now, I know you've been waiting to get to the how of all of this, and we're just about there. Everything we've covered until now is the sturdy foundation on which to build your business. Now it's time to pick your products and ask people to give you their money. The nuts and bolts of product curation, packaging, and fulfillment are up next. Get excited!

Action Steps

1. Take some time to think about and perhaps even document/journal what kind of experience you want to give your subscribers. What thoughts and feelings would you like them to have when they receive your box? Be specific. This guides everything that comes next.

Chapter 6

THE NUTS AND BOLTS OF PRODUCT CURATION, PACKAGING, AND FULFILLMENT

Every month, hundreds of people around the country receive delicious baked goods, perfectly packaged and undamaged, sent straight to their doorstep thanks to Jonica Thompson. Jonica is a baker extraordinaire and founder and CEO of Jonica's Bakery. Her love for baking started as a teenager, and she quickly became the go-to person in the lives of her friends and family members for birthday cakes and yummy treats for all occasions. She side-hustled for over 10 years before she finally decided to give it a go and open a real-life brick-and-mortar bakery.

Her journey hasn't always been easy. Along the way, Jonica had lots of starts and stops. The first time she opened a bakery, her business exploded so fast that she burnt out and wanted to quit. When someone came along asking to buy the business from her, she jumped at the chance. Fast-forward a few years, and she found herself unfulfilled in the corporate job that she took after selling that first bakery. Once again, Jonica decided maybe she'd give owning her own store a try. But this time, life got in the way and circumstances arose that made all of her plans fall through. Fast-forward one more time, and in 2021, a newly married Jonica was bored in her new town in Alabama without friends or much to do. *Maybe I'll give this one more shot*, she thought. *But this time, I'll get help and do it right.*

The idea for Jonica's Bakery Box had been on her mind since back when she started her first bakery all those years ago. She knew that there was an opportunity for so many more people to enjoy her delicious treats, if only she had the knowledge and infrastructure in place to make it happen. She had now successfully opened another bakery, this time with a team in place to help her. And she was also very pregnant. Scrolling on social media one day, laptop balanced on her baby belly, she came across one of my ads for Launch Your Box. She decided now was the time.

Jonica's journey looked a lot like many of my students featured in this book in many ways, except for one crucial element: she shipped perishables. She admitted to me once that the thought of shipping her cookies terrified her. What if they showed up crumbled? What if they were stale? A lot was riding on ensuring that her product arrived in the condition in which it was shipped.

Because she's so creative and driven, Jonica started experimenting with shipping her baked goods by different means before she launched. She tried out different box sizes, bag sizes, amounts of packing peanuts, heat-sealing methods for freshness, and distances to ship. She shipped boxes as far as Hawaii just to make sure they could make it that far. To find beta testers, she asked her audience who lived far away who would be willing to receive some baked goods in exchange for offering her feedback. Each tester box had a piece of paper with instructions for the recipient to walk through immediately, starting with a survey. One action item even included the beta testers taking pictures of the contents so Jonica could know for sure what had happened in transit.

After conducting many test boxes and tweaking her methods, she was finally satisfied that she knew how to ship baked goods thousands of miles away and have them arrive just as fresh as when they were sent. She implemented the rest of what I teach in this book, got her box launched, and she was off. Now Jonica has over 100 subscribers to her subscription box and a waitlist full of eager people hoping to get in.

For most of you, the nuts and bolts of putting your boxes together won't be quite as complicated as they were for Jonica. But the idea is the same: you want to choose products your subscribers will love and ship them in a reliable and affordable way.

You've learned how to identify your ideal customers, build an audience full of those people, create community, and know what kind of experience you're offering them. Now it's time to talk logistics.

When you look at the nuts and bolts of a subscription box business, it's about four things: products, packaging, fulfillment, and shipping. Sprinkle in a little tech, and you're on your way to building that subscription box business you've been dreaming of. Let's get into it.

PRODUCTS

It's time to have some fun! Buying products for your sub-scription boxes—choosing items you know your ideal customer will absolutely love—is one of the best parts of this business. But remember, it is a business. Here are a few of the basic things to keep in mind as we move through the chapter.

The Three P's

First and foremost, you want your business to be profitable, so it's important to know how much you can spend when sourcing products. You want your customers to love and value what they receive, so the quality and experience is equally as important. Here are three rules to keep in mind.

1. **Price.** If you already sell products, whether in a physical store or online, use those prices as a starting point for setting the price point of your box. Look at your average order value (AOV) and consider pricing your box close to that. When I started my subscription box, the average amount my customers spent per purchase was $38, so I priced my box at $40. (My prices have since gone up, but this is a great way to gauge where to start.)

    If you don't sell products yet, that's okay, you'll just need to do some market research. Look at other boxes in your niche and get a range of the lowest to the highest and pick somewhere in the middle. I don't want you to be the cheapest or the most expensive. Between those two extremes is a comfortable place to start. The thinking here is that if you price your box way too high, it's much harder to lower prices than to raise them later. But if you start too low, it's harder to afford the items you want to put in your box while remaining profitable. Now that you have a starting price point for your box, let's work on a product budget for when you begin to source products.

2. **Profit margin.** While you're sourcing products, discovering new vendors, and considering all your options, you need to keep your profit margin firmly in mind. I tell all of my first-time subscription box owners to make sure that their profit margin is at least 30 percent. Ideally, it's closer to 50 percent, but at the beginning you'll go through some trial and error, so you have time to increase your profits as you perfect this process. This means that the total of all your costs for one box—the price of all the items, packaging, and shipping—should not be more than 70 percent of the price a subscriber pays for a box.

   So, if your box costs $50, the price you pay for the products, packaging, and shipping for that box should not cost you more than $35. And again, ideally this is actually closer to $25. When I first started my box business, I struggled to be profitable because I kept wanting to add "one more thing" to each box. Wanting to delight your subscribers is a great thing to want to accomplish, but those "one more things" were eating into my profits. At a certain point, I had to draw a line, and you will need to do so as well.

MY BOX BUDGET

What do you want to charge?	
CC Processing Fee	
Cost of Product 1	
Cost of Product 2	
Cost of Product 3	
Cost of Product 4	
Cost of Product 5	
Printed Materials	
Box Cost	
Packaging Materials	
Labor	
Sales Tax	
Shipping Cost	
Total Cost of Box	
Individual Box Profit	
Percent of Profit	

3. **Perceived value.** Instead of constantly adding more small things into your boxes, consider increasing the perceived value of the box. This goes back to our discussion in Chapter 5 of creating an experience. Packaging your contents with care and presenting them nicely goes a long way in adding value.

Brand inserts on printed, well-designed card stock are also great for adding a touch to build connection and add to the customer experience of the box and individual products. Think of ways to increase the perceived value of your box before you get carried away with adding more products and realize that this business you built to help make you some money isn't actually doing that at all.

What to Choose

A lot of my subscription box students want some parameters for how to choose what items should go into their first boxes. And this is one of those times when I'll tell you, well, it's really up to you. While I can't tell you exactly what to pick, I can give you some guidelines and a quick exercise to help get you started. First, try a 60-second brain dump.

The 60-Second Brain Dump

This step is all about brainstorming quickly—literally. When I say 60 seconds, I mean 60 seconds. I like to call it speed thinking. There is no room for overthinking in this exercise. Overthinking stifles creativity and may stop a great idea from ever coming to light. This step of the process is fast and fun!

1. Set a timer for 60 seconds.

2. Grab a set of sticky notes and write down everything you can think of to put in your subscription box for month 1, keeping in mind what your ideal customer is thinking, feeling, and doing that month. Write one item on each sticky note. Place

those sticky notes on the pile for that month. Go rapid fire—think slapjack, the card game where you lay cards down fast and try to slap the jack first. Write and stick, write and stick, the faster the better. If you feel like doing a second month, great! But no pressure. We're just trying to get your first box out into the world.

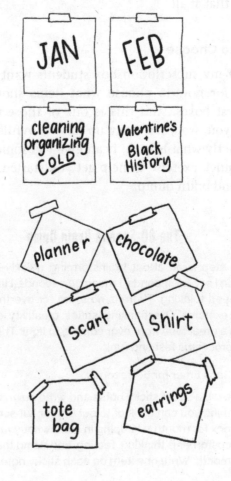

One tip for choosing what to put into your box is to create a theme for a cohesive package. Often, I find it helpful to start with a color palette. Some examples of boxes I've curated in the past include:

- Matching colors and a summer theme
- All things wild, pink, and leopard print
- Kids' summer necessities and flamingo fun

I can't tell you exactly what to put in your box, but I'll give you some guidelines for how I chose my first items that still help me make decisions to this day. Make sure you're keeping your profit margin in mind, and try out the following formula if you're stuck:

1. **Aim for three to five items.** That's the average for most subscription boxes. I want enough items so the box feels full, but not too many or they will start collecting. If a subscriber feels as if their items are starting to pile up and not getting used, they are more likely to cancel.

2. **Choose a main item for each month.** This will usually be the most expensive item or the item with the biggest value. This is the item you will build the rest of the box around and is usually worth picking first.

3. **Think about what complements the main item.** This is something that can be worn with or used with that main item. Go back to what your ideal customer is thinking, feeling, and doing. How will they use these items together?

4. **Consider something fun, something functional, something unique, and something personalized.** This might not

work for all boxes, but when I'm stuck, I use this to shake out some ideas.

5. **Keep themes and colors in mind.** You want to curate a cohesive box, one in which all the items complement each other.

Tip: If you're a complete beginner, a great way to get started might be a one-item-of-the-month box, where you provide subscribers with only one item each month. In addition to my curated Monogram Box, I also have a one-item-of-the-month subscription, my T-Shirt Club. Each month, my subscribers receive a T-shirt I've designed for them. The themes, colors, and designs are different, but every month they get a T-shirt, and they love it. There are many benefits to this kind of subscription, especially for new subscription box owners: lower barrier to get started, easier to pack and ship, and potentially higher profit margins. If you're overwhelmed by the thought of picking items, think about how easy it could be to start with just one product.

SOURCING

One of the first questions you'll face is where to buy the products you need for your box. This consumes so much of the conversation inside of my Launch Your Box membership group. The most important thing to know: do not purchase your items from a retail store or retail website. That won't work for a couple reasons. First, the price you pay there makes it impossible to profit and provide enough value to your subscribers. Retails stores mark up their prices and will be the most expensive place to shop. Second, as your subscription box business grows, you'll need to purchase large quantities of the same item, and retail stores won't be able to fill your needs.

There are many options when it comes to purchasing products. None of them is the right answer for every subscription box business to source every product they'll need. This isn't a one-size-fits-all. You'll learn a lot of this by experience, and your needs will change as you gain more subscribers. There are different right answers for different types of products at different stages in your business. In this section, I'll show you the best places to start and where I started myself.

Wholesale Sites

Whenever possible, purchase products directly from the wholesaler or manufacturer. This allows you to skip the broker, which means big savings and higher profit margins. When you purchase from a distributor or vendor, you'll be paying their price, which includes their markup. If you're looking for handmade products for your subscription box, wholesale sites are a great place to source them. These sites connect independent makers with small- to medium-sized retail businesses. On wholesale marketplaces like Faire, Tundra, and Abound, brands and retailers apply to join the platform and gain access to each other. Brands set minimum order quantities (MOQs), which can present a challenge when you're getting started, but still might be a good fit if you have enough subscribers right out of the gate. As your subscriber numbers grow, so will your buying power and ability to lower your cost per piece.

Market and Trade Shows

Attending Markets and trade shows gives you the opportunity to see products in person, meet wholesale vendors or manufacturers, and see a wide range of products in one place. Plus it's so fun! When you're sourcing products for your subscription box, I always encourage people to try Markets or trade shows if they can. It's truly an experience and sparks your creativity much more than only looking at products online. When you're part of our community, you'll hear subscription box owners talk about "going to Market." Markets are usually held in large metro areas in multistory buildings. There are Markets dedicated to specific categories of products from home decor and gifts to apparel to kids and more. Inside, you'll find floor after floor chock-full of vendor booths where you can find just about anything within your category.

The first time I went to Market was an absolute thrill. It was early days in my business, and I'd heard several of my business-owner friends talk about this magical place called Market. I knew my friends went there a few times a year to purchase products for their businesses. I asked questions and had enough details that I was dying to go. I had Market FOMO! Market sounded both magical and overwhelming, so I asked a friend of mine if I could tag along with her when she went to the Apparel Market in Dallas. I wasn't selling a lot of apparel at that time and knew the Market I really wanted to attend was the Home and Gift Market, but I also knew enough to know it was more important to go with an experienced Market buyer who could show me how things worked. If you can't, don't be discouraged. You'll be able to figure it out on your own. It just might require a little more courage and gumption to get out there and ask questions.

It turned out that the hype was real. It was magical. As soon as I stepped into Dallas Market Center, my senses were immediately taken over. Sights, sounds, and smells came at me from all directions. There was the hustle and bustle of people moving with purpose in every direction, and new things to look at everywhere I turned. It was overwhelming and exhilarating at the same time. Before we even got started, I was already hooked! It was like something out of a movie scene.

After checking in and getting our badges, my friend and I set off on a three-day adventure as we visited thousands of vendor booths in search of the perfect items. It felt like the World Wide Web was at our fingertips, but instead of having to guess what an item might really look and feel like, they were all right there in front of us. I didn't have to make a decision about a product based solely on what I could see on my computer screen. I was able to see the size of items, touch the fabrics, meet the vendors, and obtain a complete understanding of each product I considered purchasing. It was a truly unique buying experience.

I knew this was it. This was where I would find inspiration and curate all the collections for my subscription boxes. With every step I took, I found something new and different my subscribers would love. I took pictures, picked up catalogs, and slowly started to see my vision of this subscription box come to life. As my subscription business grew, I started working closely with these vendors I had met at Market. Buying for my subscription box meant purchasing large quantities of items. This gave me buying power and allowed me to obtain bulk discounts and first access to vendors' new lookbooks. Over time, some of these relationships developed further, as vendors now manufacture custom products exclusively for my subscription box. I nurtured these relationships and eventually they led to others and my network grew, both intentionally and organically.

And it all started with this one trip to Market, one vendor relationship, one product at a time, and one turned into many. I still attend Markets, though I no longer buy products for my boxes there; I go to meet new people, build relationships, and get a sense of style and trends for the upcoming seasons. Every time I go, it's a different experience, but it's always magical. It's important in this process to try not to get overwhelmed. It's easy to feel like there are endless products, companies, and people to meet. It's tempting to feel like you're bound to mess up. And you almost certainly will! But that's just part of building a business. Remember the trust and confidence we talked about in Chapter 1? You're going to show up and go for it. Everything starts with a first step. I strongly encourage you to do a search for a local Market near to you. Even if you have to travel a few hours, it's always worth it. You'll have so much fun.

Brand Websites

Buying products directly from a brand's website offers peace of mind and potential savings among other benefits. Here are several reasons why:

1. **Brand loyalty pays off.** If you are loyal to a particular brand, purchasing from them directly allows you to take advantage of any brand loyalty perks and discounts they offer.

2. **Access to a wider range of products.** Brands may not make their full line of products available to marketplaces. To see all they have to offer, head to their own website.

3. **Authenticity of product guaranteed.**
   Buying from a brand's website instead of a
   marketplace ensures you are buying genuine,
   authentic products. I haven't ever been fooled
   by a marketplace vendor, but it's always a
   small risk you take.

Global Marketplaces

Finding vendors or manufacturers to supply you with
products becomes challenging when you need 100, 500,
or even 1,000 of the same item. Many subscription box
owners, including me, choose to work directly with manufacturers, including those overseas. You might not need
to choose this route until you have more subscribers or a
few launches under your belt. But if you intend to keep
growing, it's almost guaranteed that at some point you'll
need to use a global marketplace. Global marketplaces like
Alibaba, AliExpress, and IndiaMART are websites that connect buyers and sellers.

1. **Alibaba** is a great place for small businesses
   like subscription boxes to gain an
   understanding of the sourcing process.
   You don't need special credentials to
   source through Alibaba, although most
   manufacturers do have MOQs. The vast
   majority of the manufacturers on Alibaba are
   in China, with others in Japan or India.

2. **AliExpress** is a business-to-consumer (B2C)
   website, so expect to find prices to be higher
   than on Alibaba. Some subscription box
   owners start sourcing through AliExpress
   because there are no MOQs required, and
   they can still save a lot.

3. **IndiaMART** is India's largest online business-to-business (B2B) marketplace, connecting buyers and sellers.

Making or Manufacturing Products Yourself

If you're a maker, you might want to make some of the items for your subscription box. Obviously, you won't need to find vendors or manufacturers for your products since you are the manufacturer. However, you will need to carefully consider just how many items you can reasonably produce. Inside Launch Your Box, we have members who handcraft their own soaps, candles, jewelry, custom nail polish, glitter tumblers, and so much more. Launch Your Box member Rachel Karpf of Mic Drop Miniatures even uses a 3-D printer to create the most incredible miniatures for her subscribers to use to decorate their dollhouses or miniature scenes. I'm more than a little obsessed with the miniature Frito bag she made for one of her boxes. Realize that manufacturing your own items brings its own set of challenges to growing and scaling your subscription box. It's absolutely possible to grow and scale; it just takes careful planning.

PACKAGING

Packaging is one of my favorite parts of my subscription box, and one I strongly encourage you not to neglect. I love what's inside those boxes every month—and spend a lot of time curating an amazing experience for my subscribers—but there's a lot to get excited about when it comes to packaging too. The nature of a subscription box business means you can't hand-deliver your box to each subscriber every month, although there was a period early in my business when I did do some of that.

Your box and its packaging acts as "the face" of your business and is the beginning of your subscriber's experience. That makes it worth taking the time and effort to make it special. First impressions matter. You took the time to carefully curate the products in the box, so take the time to package them thoughtfully.

> *Your box and its packaging acts as "the face" of your business and is the beginning of your subscriber's experience.*

Guidelines

I'm all about getting rid of the overwhelm, so let's keep things simple by talking about the five main things you need to consider when making packaging decisions for your subscription box:

1. **Go with a basic box.** One of the first packaging decisions you'll be faced with is whether to dress up a basic box or go all in with a custom box. I know how tempting it is to go with a custom-designed, fully branded box. However, the smart decision is to start with a basic box. It's going to take you a few months to figure out what size box is going to work best for your subscription. You don't want to invest in hundreds or thousands of custom boxes and then discover they don't fit your needs. Remember, we're focused on being profitable from the beginning. Don't make the mistake of thinking a basic box means a boring box. It's possible to dress up

your box and make it eye-catching and on-brand without spending a lot of money. You'll be amazed by the custom-like packaging you can achieve with stickers, stamps, and tape.

2. **Pick a size.** You'll need to decide what size basic box you need. It should allow for enough room for your items to fit easily but still appear "full." When a subscriber opens your box, they should never be met with a jumble of items haphazardly placed inside with a ton of room to move around. Package your items carefully and intentionally, so they look as if they were designed to go together. When deciding what size to order, think about the objects you plan to include and how much it will cost to ship. Most carriers price based on dimensional weight, so the bigger your box, the more it will cost to ship. Avoid making costly mistakes by doing your research and considering a variety of options.

3. **Consider a bag.** Not all subscriptions come in boxes. My T-shirt subscription arrives in a custom poly mailer. I call it the T-Shirt Club because it's technically not a box. You can save a ton of money using shipping bags or poly mailers. If I pack my T-shirts in a box, they weigh more than a pound. But in a poly mailer, they're less than a pound. It doesn't sound like much, but that slight difference in weight makes an immense difference in shipping costs. I'm still providing my subscribers with an on-brand, instantly recognizable package that arrives on their doorstep each month. If you're sending soft goods or apparel to your subscribers, consider whether a poly mailer could be the right decision for you.

4. **Pick your filler.** I mentioned the importance of making your box feel "full." You may have times when the items you chose so carefully don't fill your box completely, or your box contains an item that is fragile and needs to be protected during shipping. In these situations, you'll need to use some type of filler like air pillows, shreds, tissue paper, or packing peanuts. You can find filler in your brand colors to add a custom feel to the overall experience. It can also just be used to create a more carefully packaged look for your box to add to the gift-like experience. Get creative here!

5. **Use inserts.** I briefly mentioned these earlier when we talked about adding perceived value to your box. Inserts in your subscription box serve several purposes. They add to the perceived value of your box, share information about your brand, and provide any necessary extra instructions. Use your insert to guide your subscriber through the box, offering explanations or instructions if needed. This is a great opportunity to share your inspiration for the box or the reasons why you chose certain items for your subscribers. Don't be afraid to get personal. Consider adding a personalized note from time to time, simply thanking subscribers for being part of your community. And most important, don't forget to include calls to action on your inserts. Ask your subscribers to take pictures of themselves wearing or using items in the box, share them on social media, and tag you.

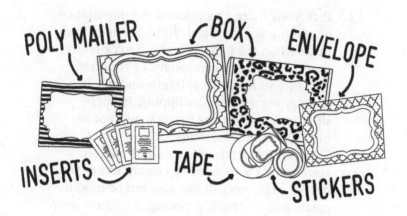

Get more packaging tips and strategies from my packaging cheat sheet at SarahsBookBonus.com.

FULFILLMENT

After nailing down your products and packaging, your next item of business is how you are going to ship them. This step in the process is referred to as fulfillment. You basically have two options to consider for fulfillment: doing it yourself or outsourcing it to another company. At the start, most small business owners choose to fulfill their own orders, whether they have one order a day from an Etsy shop or 50 a day from their own website. But as their businesses grow and the volume of orders or number of subscribers increases, their fulfillment needs change. Some subscription box owners eventually partner with fulfillment centers that handle all aspects of packing and shipping for them for a fee.

When you are brand new to selling products, the thought of packing and shipping hundreds of subscription boxes at once might feel daunting. Don't get ahead of yourself and talk yourself out of it before you even get started. I had this conversation with a new member of Launch Your Box. She had gotten herself all wound up, worrying about how she would pack hundreds of subscription boxes every month. And at this point, she hadn't even launched her box yet. She was still in the beginning stages of starting a subscription box and, honestly, she needed to focus her time and energy on building her audience. Instead of worrying about how she would pack hundreds of boxes, I gave her the same advice I'm going to give you: Think about what 50 boxes would look like. Could you manage packing 50 boxes in your current space? Then think about what might need to change if your subscriber numbers grew to 100 or 200.

When I started my subscription box, I packed the boxes for my 44 subscribers on a long cabinet in my studio. I loved that it was counter height and large enough to hold all the boxes at one time. Of course, as my subscriber numbers grew, that cabinet turned into rows of folding tables and eventually into my own warehouse. I'd always sworn I would never have a warehouse, because I didn't want to manage more stuff and more people. I even told myself I'd stop growing in order to prevent the need for a new warehouse. I couldn't have been more wrong.

The growth of my subscription box was inevitable and so was that warehouse I'd been dreading. It turns out that the warehouse was one of the best decisions I made for my business. It allowed me to grow and expand and for my team and I to be so much more efficient in everything we did.

As you grow, you'll find solutions to the space issues that will arise. Trust that you are capable of solving problems when you need to, and don't get too worked up about what is way down the road. You may start packing boxes at your kitchen table and eventually find your business and fulfillment process growing into something more than you ever imagined. Just start doing it on your own first, enlist a little help if you need it, and then move on to more advanced methods later.

The Assembly Line Method

I can honestly say that I know how to pull, package, and ship thousands of the exact same box like a breeze. Easy peasy. Time consuming, yes. But I have a system. Using an assembly line method is the most efficient way to pack. Follow the same steps in the same order for an error-free, stress-free packing experience. There are two main assembly line methods that work best for subscription box packing. Decide which one is right for you based on the space you have available and the number of items that need to be packed.

1. Set up stations of each product and push the boxes down the line, having one person at each station placing their assigned item into each box.

2. Line up a set of boxes, 10 at a time, 100 at a time, or 1,000 at a time, depending on what you have space for. Walk down the rows and drop products one at a time into each box.

Choosing one of these assembly line methods allows you to be the most efficient and make the least number of mistakes. Lo Hixson knows all about this. She's the founder of Passion & Growth, a self-care subscription box for women. She is also one of the most inspiring people you will ever meet, and I know lots of inspiring people. As a baby, Lo had a tumor on her face. It grew rapidly, which resulted in her having many surgeries throughout her childhood and young adulthood that left her with scars. She struggled seriously with self-doubt, insecurity, and limiting beliefs. She didn't believe she was worthy of anything. Finding the strength to accept and love herself didn't happen quickly or easily. A few years ago, Lo started down a path of self-development, journaling, therapy, and discovering anything and everything to help her live a joyful life. It led to a passion to help other women learn to love and accept themselves. That passion turned into a thriving subscription box business.

I love Lo's story for so many reasons. Of course, there's her ability to overcome challenges most of us will never face. I also love her fearless approach to business. When she decided to start a subscription box, she had no idea what that really meant. She knew who her ideal customer was and what kind of experience she wanted to give them—encouragement and support on their own journey to self-love. What she didn't know was how to make that happen. But in true Lo fashion, she got scrappy and figured it out.

One of my favorite parts of Lo's subscription box journey is her fulfillment story. Her first launch ended with 75 subscribers, and her subscription grew steadily each month. Lo fulfilled her subscription boxes from her two-bedroom apartment in Austin, Texas. As her subscription box grew, she kept on fulfilling from home, even when she reached 600 subscribers! Can you imagine trying to pack 600 subscription boxes filled with products from a tiny apartment? When Lo relocated to Dallas, she decided it was time to rent some warehouse space for her subscription business. Now she has more room to breathe at home and enough space to allow her subscription box business to continue to grow well beyond the 1,000-subscriber mark. Be like Lo. Start on your own, and trust that when the time is right, you'll have the resources you need to expand.

SHIPPING

Now, let's get those boxes out the door and talk shipping. This is a place where subscription box owners can end up overspending, so pay attention to that. Choosing a carrier depends on a number of factors. Not all carriers are created equal, and your shipping costs will vary from carrier to carrier based on the size and weight of your box. *Realize you can negotiate shipping prices.* Many people don't know that. Shop around to find the best service at the lowest rates. Using shipping apps and plugins can streamline the shipping process and allow you to take advantage of an already negotiated shipping rate. If you're using a fulfillment center, they may be able to get you a better shipping rate due to the volume of packages they ship.

Here are some of the basics. USPS First Class Shipping is the best way to go if your box is under 16 ounces. You won't find a carrier with rates that compare to First Class Shipping rates. If your box is over a pound, you have several different carrier options: USPS, FedEx, UPS, and every other carrier out there. Let's talk about cubic shipping, or dimensional weight. Cubic rates rely on the actual *size* of the box, not the weight. It can be heavy, but small, and ship much cheaper than you think. USPS calls this cubic shipping, while UPS and FedEx call it dim weight (dimensional weight). Using this type of shipping calculation is usually the best way to ship your boxes.

Most e-commerce platforms have shipping software attached, but if yours doesn't, or you have multiple sites, look into an online shipping software program. You can integrate all the places you sell products into one location and ship right from there. Like if I had a Shopify site, an Etsy store, and I also sold on Amazon, I could use a single shipping platform like ShipStation that would bring in all the orders from across all three selling channels. This way, I wouldn't have to log into each marketplace and set up different shipping methods. All the shipping programs have commercial pricing, which means they've negotiated a discount based on the number of users and packages as a whole—most likely a better deal than you can broker on your own. Sites like these are free, or they come with a small fee. This is a vital way for subscription box owners to cut down costs and increase profit.

My Top Shipping Rules

1. Use the smallest box you can in order to reduce the dimensional weight of your shipment. Plus remember, you don't want all that extra space anyway.

2. Integrate a shipping platform into your website to save a lot of time and money throughout the shipping process.

3. Request to chat with a local representative from your shipping carrier. They provide invaluable help when it comes to handling shipping issues and negotiating prices. Don't be afraid or embarrassed to ask questions and make friends. Connections are everything in this business.

4. Renegotiate your rates each year as your business grows. As the volume of packages you're shipping increases so does your buying power—use it.

Phew, we did it! Are you still with me? You've sourced your products, chosen your packaging, developed a fulfillment strategy, and decided on your shipping method. Look at you, you fancy pants subscription box business owner. You're really doing it. Now it's time to put it out there into the world and officially get some subscribers. Let's launch your subscription box!

> Tip: Never go into the post office or shipping center to buy postage for your subscription box. You will automatically be paying 20 to 60 percent more on postage versus using an online shipping program.

Action Steps

1. Research Markets near you to see if there is one to visit to curate products and spark creativity.

2. Try the 60-second brain dump and see what awesome ideas you can come up with in just one minute. You'll be surprised.

3. Choose a "main item" for your first box.

4. Select a few more items to complement that main item. Remember: don't go above five. And if you're really freaking out, try a one-item-a-month subscription.

5. Order some basic boxes for your first launch. Trust me—don't get fancy yet. Keep it simple.

6. Decide on your fulfillment and shipping route. Again, keep it simple. I recommend packaging them yourself in the beginning.

7. Decide on how you will create more perceived value in your box. Inserts, lovely tissue paper, stickers, and so on. Remember: don't pick anything that costs a lot. The point of this is to delight your customer while keeping your profit margins high.

Chapter 7

READY TO LAUNCH

Sarah Cummings of the Redheaded Camel started her business when she was a 19-year-old college sophomore. Her love of all things hand-lettering and art grew into a successful business that included graphic T-shirts and original artwork. No matter the medium, Sarah's designs all feature bright, happy colors, a reflection of her personality. Her goal is to spread happiness in the lives of her customers.

After several years in business, in addition to an online store selling one-off products, Sarah had three subscriptions: two T-shirt subscriptions and a hand-painted door hanger subscription. She had successfully launched the first T-shirt subscription to 60 members in a manner she describes as "flying by the seat of her pants." That subscription and her subscribers' excitement about it grew over time. Then the pandemic hit. Sarah began to lose subscribers, as people looked for ways to cut unnecessary costs during such a stressful time. As Sarah's subscriber numbers dwindled, so did her energy and enthusiasm for this subscription. She considered letting it die.

Luckily, Sarah decided to talk to me first about her T-shirt subscription and how she was feeling. I convinced her to give it one more try and go all in on a launch. Sarah agreed to bring all her energy and bubbly personality. She also set a goal of attracting 20 new subscribers as a result of the launch.

When Sarah goes all in, she goes all in. She took all she had learned inside Launch Your Box and paired it with everything she knew about what her audience wanted. She already had a somewhat neglected e-mail waitlist and started really pushing people toward it four weeks before her launch. Her efforts resulted in a significant increase in people on that waitlist, which of course translated into many more subscribers when she launched.

Sarah also amped up her engagement efforts. Every e-mail and every post contained a call to action (CTA). Some were as simple as directing the reader to a post to comment on or asking them to answer a question or give an opinion. The purpose of these CTAs was not to buy but to increase engagement and build relationships. This should sound familiar to you now. It's ringing some bells, right? Build your audience, have a waitlist, send out calls to action . . . we've been over all this before. Okay, back to Sarah.

Establishing an early bird bonus was another key part of Sarah's launch strategy (which I'll teach you about in this chapter). An early bird bonus is simply something someone receives for buying early; it's an incentive to not wait until the last minute. Sarah gave her waitlist early access to the bonus and then made it available to the public for the first 24 hours of her launch, exactly like I taught her to do. Then she opened her cart (made her box available for purchase) to the public and "the floodgates opened," as she later told me. She met her goal of 20 new subscribers in the first eight hours! But it didn't stop there. Sarah kept the momentum going by focusing on nothing but her launch during the days her cart was open.

She went live on social media with someone who had subscribed and had that subscriber share what she was most excited about and why she joined. Sarah also brought in two affiliates—people who had established audiences—who also loved graphic tees, to share about her offer. My point is, she promised to go all in, and she really did. We pulled out every tactic we could think of for that launch, both to create an infusion of cash for Sarah and also to reignite her passion for the business and prove that this was still something worth doing. She did so many things right during her launch, but possibly the most important was that she rediscovered her excitement for her subscription, and her audience felt that as a result.

Sarah ended her launch welcoming 75 new subscribers, nearly four times her goal. That is the power of launching (or relaunching) your subscription box energetically out into the world. But first things first. You might be asking yourself, *What does* launch *even mean?* To that I will say: good question. There are no dumb questions around here. In the subscription box world, a launch means when you make your subscription box available for purchase. We'll get into more details about this later in the chapter, but generally, this period is around one week, you have a set number of spots available, and you promote, promote, promote while you try to fill them. People have been waiting, you've been teasing it, and now they're finally able to sign up and give you their hard-earned dollars. It's time to make some money. There's something magical in an entrepreneur's journey when they make their first dollar from something they created themselves. I'm so excited for you to feel this incredible feeling!

SET A DATE

All right, first things first. Let's start with an easy one: set a date! If you've been audience building for at least 90 days and you have your products and packaging in mind, you're ready to set a date. I'd say give yourself 30 days to plan your launch, but don't set the date more than 60 days away or you might be tempted to procrastinate. The best launches have a buildup. Set your date and announce it to your audience. E-mail them, post on social, and let anyone and everyone know that your box will be available for purchase on that specific date. This also holds you accountable as well. Now you have to follow through.

The best launches have a buildup.

Look at your calendar and choose a five-day period to be your launch week. I always launch on Wednesdays and close on Sunday nights. Many other subscription box owners launch on Sundays and close cart on Thursdays. I choose Wednesday to Sunday based on the days sales have always been highest in my store. If you have a store, look at when you have the most sales in. And if you don't have one, pick a day with the most engagement on your posts. I recommend starting with a Wednesday or a Sunday, but the most important thing is that you simply pick a day and execute. This decision will not make or break your launch.

GET YOUR TECH SOLUTIONS IN PLACE

In order to launch your subscription box business, you need four pieces of tech in place. There are many other apps and software solutions that people use to manage their subscription box businesses that you can implement as you get fancier over time. For now, you just need these four things in place and ready to go before your launch. But the good news is you likely already have some of them! To be thorough, let's make sure you have the following:

1. **Website, or more specifically, a landing page.** A landing page is simply a single web page with one purpose. A landing page for a subscription box acts as a one-page advertisement of your subscription box with a CTA to either join the waitlist or become a subscriber. Make sure your landing page link is in all social media posts, e-mails, and so on to drive traffic to it. Until now, you've had a landing page whose CTA was to join the waitlist. Even if your full website is still in progress, having a waitlist landing page with some images and descriptions of your future box will generate some buzz for what's coming. Now it's also time to create one that asks people to officially subscribe to your box. We'll use that soon.

2. **Payment Processor.** This is a separate app that allows you to process recurring payments and is often simple to integrate. Don't be intimidated when you start researching. You can set up your payment processor in about 30 minutes. These charge month after month

automatically so you don't have to touch it, and deposit the money into your bank account. Some e-commerce platforms even have these built into the platform; otherwise, you'll need to integrate one, like Stripe. Just do some searching for popular ones out there that work with whatever website hosting and e-mail services you're using.

3. **E-mail Customer Relationship Manager (CRM).** Now this one you should have. We covered it in Chapter 3. If you've made it this far and are considering launching, but you don't have an e-mail list or aren't sending regular e-mails, turn around, sister. Back up to Chapter 3, and don't move on until you've built that foundation.

4. **Shipping software.** We covered this in the last chapter a bit. If you haven't already, it's time for you to get your shipping solutions in place. There is software built for e-commerce businesses that allows you to manage, automate, and process your orders.

WEBSITE + PAYMENT PROCESSOR + EMAIL CRM + SHIPPING SOFTWARE

A lot of the specifics of setting up your tech are out of the scope of this book. Plus I want to keep everything up to date for you, so you can always find more resources and guides on SarahsBookBonus.com. I know that tech can be a challenge. It held me back for quite a while, and I see it intimidate Launch Your Box members every day. But it doesn't have to be complicated. You can have a massively successful subscription box business with just the four tech solutions above. They aren't a big investment and there are great companies and solutions these days to help you get these things in place quickly. You just need to set aside a few hours, pour yourself some coffee, muster up your confidence, and knock it out.

A lot of people ask me how they know they're actually ready to launch. My simple answer is: if you've been audience building for 90 days and have the above four components in place, then that's it; you're ready to go.

> Tip: Test everything before you send it out to your audience and potential subscribers. Click every link and sign yourself up for payments/e-mails to make sure everything is operating like it should.

SET YOUR NUMBERS

Let's determine how many subscribers you can take in the first month. I don't recommend having no goal or set number for your first launch. That makes it nearly impossible to plan. I have seen some subscribers launch with no number in mind and just see how many people sign up. It almost always turns into a disaster. Not even because they don't have a successful launch! Often they do, and then they scramble because they had no idea how much of anything they needed, if they can get it, or how much time it will take. I am super conservative with this and recommend you be conservative as well.

When I first launched my box, my goal was 50 subscribers. But as I've described before, I had no idea what
I was doing. In fact, I had never even heard the term
"launch," so there was no intention to it at all. I tell my
members and students all the time that it was the worst
launch in history. Anyway, that goal of 50 subscribers was
a little arbitrary. It was generally based on the number of
students that attended my in-person classes. But I want
you to be even more specific. What I absolutely don't want
you to do is throw a dart at a dartboard. You want a rea-
sonable number that should leave you with enough boxes
to fill demand but not so many that you're left with a lot
of excess inventory. We're going to use both your e-mail
list and your waitlist to determine how many potential
subscribers to plan for. And we're going to do a little math.
I know, not all of us like this part! But this math is simple,
trust me. It's all about percentages.

- The average e-commerce e-mail conversion
  rate is 1 to 3 percent. That means if you send
  an e-mail selling something to a list of 1,000
  people, 10 to 30 will buy from you.

- An average subscription box waitlist
  conversion rate is 30 percent, depending on
  how hot or fresh your waitlist is. (Typically,
  the longer someone has been on your waitlist,
  the less likely they are to subscribe.) If you're
  new to this and have been audience building
  for the last 90 days, your list is pretty hot.
  If you had a previous business of some kind
  and you're trying to reinvigorate your list,
  they may be a little cooler and less interested.
  That's okay. This isn't a perfect science. Any
  waitlist is better than no waitlist. So generally,
  this means if you have 1,000 on your waitlist,
  about 300 will subscribe.

To set your numbers for your launch, simply use the following formula:

Number of people on your e-mail list x 0.02 = X

Number of people on your waitlist x 0.30 = Y

X + Y = your estimated starting amount

For example. Let's say you have an e-mail list of 2,300 and a waitlist of 800:

2,300 x 0.02 = 46

800 x 0.30 = 24

46 + 24 = 70

This calculation shows you should plan for 70 subscribers. That would be a pretty awesome first launch. There are many factors that affect the number of subscribers you will actually end up with by the end of your launch. However, using these industry averages allows you to choose a starting number you can feel comfortable with.

ORDER PRODUCTS AND PACKAGING

The details about products and packaging are in Chapter 6, but as you get ready to launch, you need to consider them again. I recommend having your products and packaging ahead of time before launching, although as I mentioned before, it is possible to order them (or have them still en route) after you launch. That said, you absolutely must have them in time to get your boxes out to subscribers before that recurring payment hits their bank account again. So within 30 days. You do not want customers to have two charges on their account without even receiving one box yet.

Set your goals and begin ordering products and packaging, or at least have conversations with vendors or manufacturers, so they are on the same timeline as you for your first few shipments. If you're a first-timer, I told you to use basic boxes for now. But if you have an established business or have done this before, just remember that custom packaging can take four to eight weeks domestically, so plan for that.

KEEP BUILDING YOUR AUDIENCE

Your audience-building efforts will ramp up during this time as well. Plan a giveaway and maybe even run some ads on social media. Most of all, now is the time to really engage with the audience you already have. Continue to serve, connect with them, and generate excitement about your upcoming launch.

Talk about your launch date nonstop while driving more traffic to your waitlist page. Remember the math we talked about in the previous section. The people on your waitlist are your warmest audience, especially right before a launch. At the end of the day, it's a numbers game.

PICK YOUR MODEL

Subscription box businesses run on one of two types of models: open or closed. There are benefits to each and reasons why one is better than the other for different types of subscription boxes at different times. For a subscription box newbie, I always recommend an open model to begin as you ramp up your business, but I'll describe both below so you know all options available to you.

Open Model

An open subscription model simply means your subscription box is open to new subscribers all the time. Subscribers can join at any time. My open subscription is my T-Shirt Club.

Recommended for:

- **Brand-new subscription boxes.** I recommend keeping your new subscription box open for at least the first three to six months.

- **Subscriptions with items that are easy to get.** This includes those you make yourself. I can get T-shirts for my subscription the next day. After that, it's as easy as printing that month's design on them and they're ready to go. I don't need to worry about planning for lead time.

- **Low-dollar subscriptions.** This especially goes for those that may lead to higher dollar subscriptions. My T-Shirt Club has a much lower cost than my Monogram Box. When a subscriber joins the T-Shirt Club, they may upgrade to a Monogram Box in the future.

Benefits:

- You are adding new subscribers all the time. You don't have to put them on a waitlist and then work to convert them later.

- You don't have to launch regularly in order to build up your subscriber base. Getting into a monthly launch cycle can feel exhausting to business owners, especially new ones.

Closed Model

With a closed subscription model, customers are only allowed to subscribe at certain times, typically during a launch.

Recommended for:

- **Seasoned subscription boxes.** Those who have been open for at least three to six months.

- **Boxes that include products that require lead times.** Items that are sourced or manufactured specially for subscription boxes require lead time. Having a closed model means you can order the quantity you need with confidence, knowing you'll have enough of each item. This is where I am now in my subscription box business, so I opt for a closed model.

- **Declining subscriber numbers.** A subscription that has been open for several months or more may start to see declining numbers. This doesn't mean you're doing anything wrong. A closed model can incentivize subscribers to stay, knowing that if they cancel, they'll have to wait for the next launch to resubscribe.

Benefits:

- You'll see a larger increase of subscribers at one time during a launch.

- A closed model gives people a reason to take action and subscribe now.

- You know exactly how much product to plan for each month.

- It allows you to create feelings of scarcity and exclusivity.

Again, I recommend all new subscription boxes start with an open model, but it's important to understand the difference between the two and which may be right for you as your subscription box business grows.

DETERMINE YOUR EARLY BIRD BONUS

An early bird bonus is used to incentivize people to take action, to sign up on the first day. Sarah used this tactic in the story at the start of this chapter. If someone is thinking about signing up and decides, "Oh, I'll come back to this later," chances are high they'll get distracted and forget about it. Everyone is so busy and pulled in many different directions. It's the function of the early bird bonus to give someone a reason to sign up now.

An early bird bonus can be either a physical or digital product. Since my subscription is a physical product, my early bird bonus is always an additional physical product. I know that in the previous chapter I talked about not getting carried away by constantly adding "one more little thing" to your boxes, and I meant it. The early bird bonus is not that. It is one more item, but it's an important one that serves a purpose. You'll do this once to incentivize sign-ups, and then it's over. Whatever you curated for that month, it's important that your early bird bonus matches and adds to the overall experience.

> *Tip: Your current subscribers will also receive the early bird bonus. You never want them to feel left out or as if they are less valuable to you than a new subscriber. This early bird bonus is a retention strategy for current subscribers.*

Keep your profit margins in mind (always), but my general rule of thumb is to keep the cost of the early bird bonus item to 10% or less of your box price.

Here are some ideas:

- Earrings or jewelry
- Socks or scarves
- Paint or brushes
- Small signs or magnets
- 8 × 10 print or card
- Exclusive stickers

My 5-Step Early Bird Bonus Strategy

1. Send the early bird offer to your e-mail waitlist the day before you open the cart (allow people to purchase). Include a picture.

2. Make sure they understand they are the first to get a chance to subscribe, and if they subscribe in the next 24 hours, they will receive the early bird bonus item.

3. Run an ad targeted to only the people on the wait-list. This can be an image, but I love a short video. Talk as if you are talking to one person.

4. On open cart day, talk about the bonus in the first live video you do on social media that morning. Show them the item and make sure they know they have to sign up that day.

5. Post the early bird offer on your page and in your stories on open cart day.

LET'S GET PREPPING (30 DAYS BEFORE)

During the 30-day period leading up to the launch, your focus needs to be on being as prepared as possible. Prepping now means less stress later. There will be enough to do during launch week. Plus you'll be nervous and anxious and all the things (which is normal!). Getting as much done ahead of time as possible will help it go smoothly.

Create everything you need before the launch, so you don't lose steam during it:

1. **Graphics and videos for posts and ads.**
   Make them now so you don't get behind.

2. **E-mails.** Write them now (more below). Don't
   wait until you are in launch mode to put
   these together.

3. **Plan your live videos.** Create a schedule and
   decide when and how you want to show up
   during launch week.

During this pre-launch period, your CTA is to join the waitlist—always, always, always. Every post, e-mail, video, and ad need to direct people to your waitlist. Remember that 30 percent. Increase those numbers!

Your to-dos during this period are all about generating excitement and growing your waitlist:

1. **Promote your waitlist.** Make a graphic and
   pin it to the top of your social media account.
   Run an ad to your waitlist.

2. **Lead magnet.** I mentioned these in Chapter
   3 about building an audience, so revisit that
   if you need a reminder. Run social media ads
   featuring your lead magnet.

3. **Go live.** Nothing will give you more juice! Go live as much as you can during this pre-launch period.

4. **E-mails.** Send one e-mail per week telling a story, highlighting a product, or sharing a review.

LAUNCH WEEK

It's launch week! This is your opportunity to shine. We'll get into my exact launch-week plan with all the nitty-gritty details, but before we do that, here are my two top launch-week tips:

1. First, prepare yourself in every way: mentally, physically, emotionally, spiritually. You'll need all of your energy and smarts this week, so take care of yourself and do what you need to do to get pumped. Try to come into launch week rested and ready. You're going to be "on" for five days straight, showing up for your audience over and over again. Launching requires a lot of physical and mental energy. Have your plan set for each day and work that plan.

2. Second, and perhaps most important, don't forget to ask for the sale. That might sound like a weird thing to say, but so many times we don't actually ask people to buy! We get nervous or feel like a slimy salesperson, but if we don't ask for the sale, we leave uncertainty in their minds. You've worked so hard, care about your customers, and know how awesome your products are. Just ask people to subscribe and be confident you can deliver.

You're going to mess up somewhere that week. We're all human, and it's bound to happen. But if you take care of yourself so you can give it your all and ask people to buy, you're off to a great start.

During launch week, along with the excitement and adrenaline, there will be a pit in your stomach. This is normal, and it's okay. It's just a sign that you care deeply. No matter how many times you launch, that feeling never goes away. I still get it every time. Launch after launch, I still wonder: *Will my audience show up? Will they buy my box? Am I good enough? Can I do this?*

When I first launched my subscription box, I had spent so much time dreaming about that day. Remember, I'd thought about starting one for 18 months before I finally did. I had spent months researching subscription boxes in my niche, identifying exactly who my ideal customer was, and choosing products with her firmly in mind. I'd even found a way to tackle the tech. By all accounts, I was ready. I was so sure I'd created something my customers would love.

But what if they didn't? my brain kept asking me. I was ready, but I was also terrified. It didn't matter how much time I'd put into planning this subscription box. It didn't matter how sure I was that my customers were going to love it. Nothing could quiet the voice in my head that kept saying, *What if nobody buys?*

I stared at the boxes I'd worked so hard to curate for my busy Southern moms. Inside each one was something fun, something functional, and something my customer wouldn't think to buy for herself. My first box had a Lilly Pulitzer tumbler, matching zipper bag with monogram, and the cutest set of custom wraps for my subscribers' phone chargers. I wanted each of my subscribers to feel seen and cared for. I knew my boxes would do exactly that. *But what if no one bought them?* I thought again. No one would ever know how amazing those boxes were.

Looking back, and after coaching hundreds of other subscription box owners in the following years, I feel a lot of compassion for myself. I also now happen to have the answer for the "newbie business owner nerves." It is: have a good first launch. You know this story already, but my launch resulted in 44 subscribers initially. I didn't even hit my goal of 50 and I was still thrilled! Within the first couple weeks, I hit it, but not at first.

Gaining subscribers and hearing them express how much they love what you send them is the best way to build your business confidence. Get out there and prove to yourself that you can do this. I promise, it's the most amazing feeling. When you're ready to launch, even if you've done everything I'm teaching you to do, it's almost inevitable that you'll have all the same worries I did. Be ready for those feelings and don't let them derail you. If you've done all the work, you are ready. You've worked so hard behind closed doors on your subscription box and it's finally time to show it to the world. You are good enough and worthy of a successful launch. Getting some customers and earning some real dollars will do wonders for your confidence moving forward. Now, let's talk about how. . . .

Five-Day Launch Plan

All right, team. Here's how this works. Following is your basic five-day launch plan:

Your Launch Week

- Day 1: Early Bird Day (for waitlist only to purchase)

- Day 2: Open Cart Day 1 (all others can purchase)

- Day 3: Open Cart Day 2

- Day 4: Open Cart Day 3

- Day 5: Close Cart Day

LAUNCH WEEK SCHEDULE

SUNDAY	MONDAY	TUESDAY	WEDNESDAY	THURSDAY	FRIDAY	SATURDAY
			early bird bonus	open Cart day 1	open Cart day 2 2	open Cart day 3 3
open Cart day 4 4	close cart day 5					

Scarcity, Urgency, and Exclusivity

In everything that you do this week—post on social media, e-mail, live videos—I want you to think about these three things you're trying to communicate to your audience about your subscription box: scarcity, urgency, and exclusivity.

Create scarcity by letting your audience know that you only have a limited number of spots available. You likely are operating with an open model, but it's true that you don't have an unlimited number of boxes for this launch. Communicate that to your audience. When I have subscribers cancel (and yes, cancellations are part of a subscription box business), I open those spots up to my waitlist first. I send an e-mail letting them know a limited number of spots just opened. Within a few hours, those spots are always filled. Letting your audience know you have limited quantities inspires them to act.

Create urgency with a short launch window. This is why our launch is only a few days long. It lets people know they need to take action and subscribe, because the opportunity isn't going to last long. This is also the reason for the early bird bonus. Get your audience to buy now, not later.

Create a sense of exclusivity by designing or sourcing items for your subscription boxes that are only available to subscribers. When you do your live box openings, share those items and let viewers know they are exclusively for subscription box members. This generates powerful feelings of FOMO. And feelings of FOMO are strong motivators that turn people on your waitlist into subscribers.

Social Posts

Post three times a day, every day, on social media during your launch week. I recommend posting morning, noon, and night. That makes it easy. Everything you post during this five-day period is about your subscription! The CTA on every post is to purchase your box. Include a link to join your subscription on every post. It's time to practice asking for the sale.

Your posts should include:

1. **Benefits.** Don't just talk about the items in your box. Talk about their benefits. Exclusive designs, first access, discounts, convenience, quality, and so on. A good way to think about the difference between a description of the item and its benefits is this: a cute, pink T-shirt versus a cute, pink T-shirt that comes straight to your door, handpicked for you, that makes you feel confident and put together, even when you only have five minutes in the morning.

2. **Reviews.** Admittedly, this is a little tough to come by if this is your first month sending out a box, but you can still post comments from subscribers about how excited they are about the products and remarks about any sneak peeks you've offered. If you have past boxes or products, then post reviews from those. We're trying to create a little FOMO here and make people "want in."

3. **Video clips.** Record and post short video clips of you talking about your subscription box, showing the box, making a product, modeling something, and so on. Any of the ideas I talked about for your live videos in Chapter 3 will work well here.

4. **Behind the scenes.** People love to see what you have going on. Have you ever heard that people buy things from people that they know, like, and trust? It's a common and cliché phrase in business, but it's absolutely true. Letting people in on what's going on behind the camera is a great way to build

that. This doesn't have to be anything elaborate. Just be a normal person and post what you have going on. People will be much more interested than you think.

5. **Engagement.** Ask a question and get opinions. Anything that encourages people to like or comment on your posts is great this week, as it will help with the algorithm, get more eyes on your posts, and keep you top of mind for people.

6. **Go live every day.** You knew this was coming. Increase those views! People love live video, so get on there and sell. Talk about your subscription nonstop, and if you think you've talked about it enough, talk about it some more.

> *Tip: Yes, these are the types of posts you should be doing all year long. You're just doing a lot more of them this week with a specific CTA to become a subscriber.*

E-mails

E-mails are a huge part of your launch. You'll be sending out a lot of e-mails this week, each with a specific purpose. The CTA for every e-mail is to become a subscriber, obviously.

This is going to seem like a lot of e-mails. And it is. There are good reasons for that. First, every time you send an e-mail, you'll see sales come in. This is true for me every single time. I know my numbers so well now that when I have spots on my waitlist open up I can predict almost exactly how many more people I can get with a single e-mail. People read the e-mails and a percentage of them take action. Second, you'll notice below that not all the e-mails go to everyone. Your waitlist receives more e-mails than people on your regular e-mail list. Your waitlist is full of people who have told you they are interested in your subscription box. Those are the people you want to talk to and nurture the most.

E-mail 1: Goes out the day before Launch Day

- An e-mail goes out to your **waitlist only,** announcing the early bird bonus and inviting them to become subscribers. Your waitlist gets 24 hours to join before everyone else and 48 hours to grab the early bird bonus.

E-mail 2: Goes out the morning of Open Cart Day

- An e-mail goes out to your entire list and your waitlist, announcing the early bird bonus and inviting them to become subscribers.

E-mail 3: Goes out the evening of Open Cart Day

- An e-mail goes out to your entire list and your waitlist that is different from the morning e-mail. This is their last chance to grab the early bird bonus. Let them know it goes away at midnight. Create urgency and scarcity.

E-mail 4: Goes out on Open Cart Day 2

- An e-mail goes out to your waitlist only, talking about the benefits of your subscription and using stories to bust any objections people may have.

E-mail 5: Goes out on Open Cart Day 3

- An e-mail goes out to your entire list and your waitlist telling subscriber stories.

E-mail 6: Goes out on the morning of Close Cart Day

- An e-mail goes out to everyone announcing this is the last day to join.

E-mail 7: Goes out on the afternoon of Close Cart Day

- An e-mail goes out to your waitlist reminding them your cart is closing soon.

E-mail 8: Goes out the evening of Close Cart Day

- An e-mail goes out to your entire list and your waitlist letting them know this is their last chance to join.

> *Tip: To avoid over-e-mailing, once someone subscribes, set up a "subscriber" sublist in your CRM, so that they are excluded from the rest of the launch-week e-mails. Most e-mail software has easy ways to segment and tag these people.*

Get Personal

Betsy Goodman of B Goods Lettering is a member of Launch Your Box and the creator of some of the most beautiful hand-lettering you've ever seen. Before her subscription box, Betsy had an existing stationery and wax seal shop, and she also taught lettering online and through local workshops. The idea for a subscription box came to her when she realized the ongoing practice her hand-lettering students needed would be more fun if they had actual projects to complete instead of just the standard practice sheets. First, she tried a one-time Valentine box, and it was a colossal success.

Then she decided to start a regular subscription box, joined Launch Your Box, and made it happen. Three days into her first launch, Betsy posted a question in our group.

She had gotten some subscribers on open cart day and wanted to know how to keep the momentum going. Instead of simply answering her question, I invited Betsy onto the podcast for an impromptu coaching session. You can find that coaching session in episode 39 of the Launch Your Box Podcast. She was already doing a number of things right: She'd built up a waitlist that she continued to drive people to and had done a giveaway; she posted regularly on the social media platform where her ideal customer hangs out, driving people to her waitlist with posts teasing her box. I gave her some advice about going live, being visible, and sharing more about her product. But there's one additional thing I encouraged Betsy to do, and I'll encourage you to do as well, that made a big difference in her launch.

People want to hear why you are so passionate about what you do.

I told Betsy to share her story. People want to hear why you are so passionate about what you do. Tell them why you started your business; tell them why you care about them. All the tactical stuff I explained earlier in this chapter is important, *but your story and passion are the heart of your business.* Just like I had to learn years ago at that mastermind, you, too, are the influencer of your business. Let them get to know you. My subscribers don't just care that my monogrammed items and T-shirts are cute, they care about why I chose them. They care about the backstory of why I started this business especially for them. Never underestimate this kind of connection marketing, especially during launch week. Talk about your box, but don't forget to talk about you as well. When Betsy closed the cart that week, she had doubled her number of subscribers. Within a year, her subscriber numbers had grown by nearly 10 times.

SHOW UP JUST AS YOU ARE

When I was launching my higher-level coaching program, Scale Your Box, I decided to try something a little different to close out my launch. Most purchases come on the first day of the launch and on cart close day. I tell all of my clients that cart close day is when you need to bring it. It's your last push, your last chance to convince people who are on the fence to sign up.

I always go live on the evening of the last day of my launches, usually from my office. I have my hair styled (my armor) and a cute outfit and accessories on to boost my confidence. This particular launch happened to coincide with one of my daughter's weekend soccer tournaments. That meant I would be coming home after a long, hot day in the sun—tired and sweaty. Instead of shying away from that, rushing to cover up the evidence of that day, I embraced it. I showed up sunburned, sweaty, and real. Instead of running down to my office to record from the environment my audience was used to, I decided to go live from my laundry room. Honestly, it was the only quiet place in my house.

During that laundry room live, I took my audience through my launch, giving them what amounted to a masterclass in launching. I leveled with them and said what I'd done that day. I didn't have time to get all fixed up and make it to my office. But that's not what matters. I showed up regardless and gave it my best, in the midst of my real, messy, beautiful life. I have kids and a family, and they're my world. I run a business that fits into my everyday life.

Sometimes those things bump up against each other, but that's just part of it. My audience was able to relate and connect with that. I showed up as a tired mom who had spent the day running around and cheering on my child, which is the exact same thing so many women in my audience had also done that day. My original launch plan didn't include a live from my laundry room, but it ended up being one of the best launch-week decisions I've made.

You can do this. You don't have to do it perfectly, just follow the plan I laid out and show up, just as you are, and give it your all. Launch week is hard but exhilarating! In the next chapter we'll get into how to keep the momentum going and what to do next. You have to pack up and ship out the boxes to all your lovely new subscribers. You have a real business now, friends. Congrats!

Action Steps

1. Set a date to begin your five-day launch week. I recommend picking a Wednesday or Sunday.

2. Run through your tech list. Do you have a landing page for your waitlist and subscription box sign-up? Do you have a payment process? Have you decided on your shipping software?

3. With your subscriber goal in mind, order your products and packaging, or at least make plans to procure them shortly.

4. Write all of your e-mails for launch week.

5. Schedule all of your social posts and live videos for launch week.

6. Decide on your subscription model. (Hint: if you're a first-timer, go with an open model.)

7. Determine your early bird bonus.

8. Post, post, and post again.

9. Ask for the sale at every turn. That CTA everywhere is: sign up for my subscription box.

10. Don't forget to show up just as you are and give it everything. Have a great launch!

Chapter 8

FROM BOX REVEALS TO CUSTOMER CARE

You just launched a subscription box! Can you believe it?!
I can. I knew you could do it. As I'm sure you know, the
work has only begun. But before we move on, I want you
to do something to celebrate. Go out to dinner, take a nice
bath, have a glass of wine, or even just sit quietly by yourself if that's what feels right to you. Whatever it is, please
take a moment to be proud of your accomplishment, no
matter how your launch went. Launching a subscription
box business is so fun . . . and so hard. You are amazing.
Please celebrate yourself for a moment. And then, rest. I'm
sure you're exhausted. I know I am every time I launch.
Get a good night's sleep and take a day off.

After you've celebrated and rested, it's time to get to
work. You took an idea, a dream, and turned it into a reality. Your journey has just begun. A launch builds a lot of
excitement, and it's important not to let the momentum

you built up fade away. Continue doing things that keep it in the forefront. I won't harp on this because we've covered it enough already, but post in your normal rhythm to social media. Often we think people are sick of hearing about our subscription box on our platforms, so we stop talking about it, especially after a launch. We feel like that's all we've done for a week. But we must build on that momentum going into the next month so our subscribers remain excited about what's coming to their door.

Someone who does this incredibly well is Launch Your Box member Tracy of Miss Tracy Creates. She is also one of the absolute best examples of something you learned in Chapter 2: the riches are in the niches. Tracy has a napkin subscription box. Yup, just napkins. She has created a fun, unique genre of art that she calls "napkin art," where she teaches her subscribers to create cool projects with leftover napkins. You know those huge packs of novelty napkins you bought for a party when you only needed 10? Tracy carefully curates an assortment of different styles like those, sends them to her subscribers, and then throughout the rest of the month, teaches them how to use the napkins to make unique projects.

These videos and trainings create momentum and help retain and gain subscribers because customers are actually consuming the goods they've been sent. Tracy also created a private group where subscribers could show off their napkin crafts and encourage others to do theirs if they haven't already. And then, of course, when they're done, they want more! One of the worst things that can happen is your subscribers let your products stack up around their house and never even use them. When our subscribers use and enjoy the contents of their box, it creates so much excitement and anticipation for next month.

This is one of my favorite parts of having a subscription box business—each month is new and fresh. Each month I curate a box of new items I know my subscribers will love and spend time and energy reminding them how awesome it is, how much they enjoy being a subscriber, and how much value my subscription box brings to their lives. Things are never boring with this kind of business.

Until now, your focus has been on gaining subscribers. And, of course, you still want to increase your subscriber number. But right now, immediately after your launch, your focus should shift to the people who purchased your subscription box. You worked so hard to get subscribers, and now it's time to put some of that effort and attention toward retaining them. Plus, bonus: this focus on retaining the subscribers you have will naturally create enough buzz to attract the next subscribers. Let's dive into what to do in the week after you close your cart.

SEND OUT YOUR BOXES

The first next step is to send out your boxes. If for some reason you're still waiting for a product or piece of packaging to come in, you don't necessarily have to do it within a week of your launch ending. But as I said earlier, you absolutely must ensure that those packages arrive before the next payment runs (within 30 days). I recommend that you send them out as soon as you possibly can because people are excited. Do it so that you can both reward your subscribers and get it off your plate. Refer to Chapter 6 for some tips about assembling and shipping.

CREATE EXCITEMENT AND FOMO WITH A BOX REVEAL

People love watching unboxing videos. They are always some of my most viewed videos. You've heard me mention them before in this book, and if you just launched for the first time, you finally have a box to reveal! They are a way for you to create feelings of excitement and community among your subscribers and serious FOMO among the rest of your audience. Take a little time to plan your unboxing, to give your audience who hasn't subscribed yet a sense of what it's like to receive your box and connect further with those who have subscribed.

Set a Date

Choose a date for your box reveal, put it on your calendar, and announce it to your followers. The more people who show up to watch live, the better the experience will be for everyone. Setting a date allows you to build excitement and anticipation and helps people plan to be there. Every time you share a sneak peek or behind-the-scenes view on social media, share the live unboxing date.

I wait until 90 percent of my boxes show as delivered inside my shipping platform before I schedule a box reveal in order to preserve the surprise for my subscribers. I'd hate for someone to show up who hasn't received their box and have the contents spoiled for them. (Although, the title and purpose of the video is clear, so honestly maybe that's on them.) Evenings or weekends are usually best, when you know most of your subscribers are available.

Set the Stage

Stage an inviting background. Stack your subscription boxes behind you or items that are relative to your subscription. Make it fun. You don't want to have a blank wall behind you sitting in a dark, dingy room. Make sure you have good lighting and good placement for your camera. You don't need heavy or fancy equipment here. I just use my cell phone or tablet and a ring light. Dress to coordinate with the box. If there is clothing inside your subscription, wear it! I often wear the T-shirt that is in the box I am revealing.

Elements of a Live Box Reveal

In Chapter 3 we reviewed some elements of a successful live video. Here I'm going to do something similar, but this time these tips are specific to a live box reveal. These videos are important enough that they deserve their own instructions:

1. **Encourage engagement early.** Once you press that button to record, bring lots of energy. Introduce yourself immediately and welcome everyone who is there with you. Encourage those watching to engage in the comments. Ask questions like the ones that follow to jump-start the conversation:

    - Are you a subscriber?

    - Did you receive your subscription box?

    - What is your favorite part of the box?

    - What products have you used so far?

2. **State your hook.** Viewers decide within the first 15 seconds whether to stay or to continue to scroll down their feed. So within those first 15 seconds, state the hook of your video. In this case, your hook is that you're revealing the contents of your subscription box that month. That alone is a great hook. People are always curious about what's in your subscription box. Let your audience know what you'll be talking about and why it matters to them. You could also mention some ways you'll be showcasing how to use the items. It's worth practicing your hook so you can say it confidently and quickly. It can be something as simple as, "I'm so glad you're here! Today we're going to be unboxing September's Monogram Box."

3. **Tell the story of the box.** Followers like to know the story behind your box. Tell them about your inspiration and why you curated this box especially for your subscribers. Give some insight into the behind-the-scenes. Talk about where you source any unusual pieces from or how you designed custom-made items. This is your opportunity to talk about what makes your box unique. Big box companies don't do this—they're not curated by a single person with the thoughtfulness that you have. Don't simply whip open your subscription box and say, "Look at this," and then be done. Tell the story of the box and each item, and offer your audience the experience you want them to feel when they receive their box each month.

4. **Get excited!** Before you start opening the
   box, get yourself hyped. Quite simply, your
   audience doesn't want a boring video that
   lacks energy. Your box is something worth
   getting excited about, so exude that. Your
   subscribers are thrilled to get their boxes and
   watch the video, so feed off their enthusiasm.
   Throughout the video, engage with your
   followers, and talk with people in the
   chat. During my box reveals, I speak to the
   viewers. Build that community we discussed
   in Chapter 5 and let your excitement be
   contagious.

5. **Unbox and show off all the items.** Now
   the fun begins! I usually start with the
   smaller bits included in my box to build up
   to larger or more valuable items. I tell a little
   story about each piece and share how they
   coordinate and can be used. For instance,
   if you have clothing or jewelry, share a few
   styling tips or outfit ideas. Take your time on
   each item. You chose these items on purpose
   with your ideal customers in mind. Show
   them off! You likely love them as well, so
   let that passion show and be proud of these
   intentional pieces you picked. Style them,
   use them, open them, consume them. Get
   creative here and help your subscribers
   envision using them in their own lives.

6. **Call to action (CTA).** Always include a CTA. Send your audience to a sales page, waitlist, or opt-in. Occasionally, I offer a free downloadable during my unboxing. I often include a printed quote inside my box, and I can take that, or the theme of the box, and make a cute 8 x 10 downloadable print or cellphone wallpaper and offer it as a free gift when people join my e-mail list. Or if you feel like going for it and you have an open model for subscription, you can always send them right to your sales page and ask them to sign up. There is some experimentation required here, and over time you'll understand what works best for you and your audience. Try things out. But always, always have a CTA and have it be in e-mail in some way.

7. **Bonus: sneak peek at next month's box.** If this was your first launch and you could barely think past month one, don't worry too much about this. But if you already have some products on hand or in mind for your second box, add in a quick sneak peek at the end of your unboxing video. I typically use a zoomed-in image that gives them an idea of the color palette or hints at the theme.

ELEMENTS OF A
LIVE UNBOXING

- encourage engagement early
- state your hook
- tell the story of the box
- get excited
- unbox & show off
- give a CTA
- sneak peek

After the Video Unboxing

When you're done with your live video, it's time to get as much use out of it as you can. You went through all the effort of creating it, and your subscribers enjoyed it. Here are five ways to repurpose your unboxing:

1. **Write a quick e-mail, encouraging readers to click over to watch a replay of the video unboxing.** Include a few pictures, and link the video to entice them to view it. Quick tip: this e-mail carries the same format as the video. Your subject line is the hook. Share a short story in the first paragraph, then tell

readers what items came in the box, why you chose them, and how they go together. Then use the same CTA from the video.

2. **Schedule three to four social media posts for the week using clips or pictures of the unboxing and encourage people to go watch it.** You could use the same tactic for the e-mail here and share a cute story to hook the reader or mention a few comments from viewers who loved it.

3. **Create a blog post for your website.** Take pictures of the unboxing and create a post about it with only pictures and text. Not everyone likes to watch videos, so this provides a different method for your audience to consume the unboxing.

4. **Create Pinterest pins.** These pins are designed to drive traffic back to the blog post about the unboxing. I actually have templates for these pins and just change up the graphic and link every time I promote a new unboxing post. If you don't use a blog, you could always just have your pins link to your subscription box sales page.

5. **Create short videos for formats like Instagram Reels, TikTok, YouTube Shorts, or any medium that uses quick videos.** These could be a sped-up version of the entire unboxing, perhaps with a voice-over or text on it, or maybe use a particularly engaging clip of the unboxing video.

HELP SUBSCRIBERS CONSUME THE CONTENTS OF YOUR BOX

An important part of your subscriber retention plan needs to be helping your subscribers consume the contents of their box. If they don't, after a few months those subscription boxes may start to pile up. And if a subscriber feels they're not able to use what's in the boxes quickly, they are likely to cancel. Find ways to help your subscribers consume the products. Obviously this is easier if your subscription is a tea of the month, gourmet sweet treats for people or their pets, or even a candle or soap. When your subscription box items aren't actually "consumable," you need to help your subscribers use what's in the box so they continue to see the value. Use social media posts and e-mails to show your subscribers how they can use the items you chose especially for them.

Launch Your Box member Kristy Bottle, of Kristy's Craft Room, does this very well. Her subscribers receive a kit to complete a craft each month. Kristy goes live and completes the crafts along with her subscribers, teaching them and building community and belonging. Knowing they can hop on a live with Kristy or watch a replay at their convenience makes it more likely that Kristy's subscribers will take the time to make the craft rather than setting the box aside for later and forgetting about it until the next month's box shows up.

Amanda Stucky, who you met in Chapter 2, doesn't just send her subscribers a box of stickers and accessories for the Hobonichi planners each month. She goes live and plans alongside them, using those same stickers in her own planner. She helps her subscribers consume the contents of the box, which helps them see the value and stay subscribed.

I help my subscribers consume the contents of their subscriptions every month by publishing a style guide blog, showing several different ways they can wear that month's T-shirt. I include casual, dressed-up, and trendy looks to show them how versatile the tee is. I also love to post when I'm using products from the subscription box and talk about how I'm using them. I even do this with past boxes. So if I'm headed to a soccer game and I have the bag that came in last November's box in my trunk, I'll take a quick picture of it with everything I have loaded into it and turn the picture into a social media post. I'm showing my audience that I send items they can use and enjoy for a long time. If they take an item out of the box and it goes in the closet and they never use it, or they use it one time and never come back and use it, they'll start to feel like they're wasting their money. I include a shout-out to my subscribers and ask who else has this bag.

Use those subscriber responses to show others how to use an item in different ways than maybe they had originally planned so they can feel good about their purchases. This makes for great social media content. Once a subscriber texted me, "I'm going to Disneyland and I've got my sling bag from the February box, and the T-shirt from the January box, and the hat from the October box! I'm ready to go!" I loved that. After I asked her if I could share her message on my page, I created a quick post saying, "Here's Deborah headed off to Disney with her Framed gear!" I'm reminding them that they have those items so they can pull them out and use them. People feel good as consumers when they get a lot of use out of something they purchased.

ENCOURAGE SUBSCRIBERS TO SHARE

The only thing better than you promoting your box is your subscribers doing it for you. Encourage your subscribers to share their boxes online—or even to do their own unboxings! Once they start receiving their boxes, they'll want to share their excitement with you and with their family and friends. You'll get direct messages and be tagged in posts where they say things like, "Oh my gosh! This is my favorite box ever!" I receive those messages every month, and they light me up. Even after all these years, I know I've curated something amazing, but I never know how it's going to be received. One of the best parts of this business is seeing others' excitement when their products arrive. It takes me back to the days of sitting in my store, watching people open the boxes in their cars parked right out front. These messages will make you feel great and provide you with the validation that all your hard work has paid off.

They're also valuable marketing tools. When those messages and e-mails start coming in and I'm tagged in comments on social media, I'm able to share them with my audience in a way that makes other subscribers feel excited too. When you share early comments, it creates more excitement for the subscribers whose boxes haven't arrived yet. You're creating more anticipation for current subscribers and FOMO for those people who don't yet subscribe. Used correctly, this type of social proof makes nonsubscribers feel regretful that they didn't subscribe in time to get that month's box and pushes them to consider becoming a subscriber.

The only thing better than you promoting your box is your subscribers doing it for you.

The bottom line is, when subscribers share their excitement about your box, turn it into content. After you get their permission, turn those pictures, comments, and messages into graphics to share on your social media channels. This type of social proof is incredibly valuable. Your audience will respond to subscribers they identify with, telling them what your box means to them and why it's worth the cost.

GET THEM EXCITED FOR NEXT MONTH

As soon as the current month's box has shipped, it's time to start building excitement for the next box. I already mentioned adding in a sneak peek of next month's box. That's a fun way to create some curiosity and excitement. Several members of Launch Your Box add something to their subscription boxes that serves as a clue for what's in the next month's box. This is a great retention tactic. It gets subscribers excited and intrigued about what's coming next month.

Britney of the Brainfetti Box (Chapter 3) does this very well. One of her boxes included a little notepad that said, "A hint of things to come." It was decorated in pride month colors. It was meant to hint to her subscribers that the next box was going to focus on organization and LGBTQ pride. She didn't tell them too much; the box contents were still a surprise, but she told them enough to generate excitement and curiosity. It's like a Goldilocks hint: not too much, not too little, but *just* right.

PROVIDE EXCEPTIONAL CUSTOMER CARE

You will likely have shipping and quality issues sometimes. They happen to everyone and come with the territory. Even with all the necessary quality-control processes in place, things will occasionally go wrong. Every time they do, you have the opportunity to handle these issues in a way that not only satisfies your subscriber but also deepens the relationship and makes them more likely to remain a subscriber longer. Customer care cannot be an afterthought. As small businesses, we have to remember that our subscribers are people and provide customer service that takes it to the next level. I think of it more like a customer concierge. There needs to be white-glove service for your subscribers. Making exceptional customer care a priority is good practice as a major retention strategy, and, more important, part of treating people well and the way you'd like to be treated.

If I send out 3,000 T-shirts to my T-Shirt Club members, there might be a small hole in four of them. My team does their best to catch issues like this as they're folding and packing the shirts. But if the hole is in a spot that makes it hard to detect, a few could make it out the door. When something like this happens, it's important to have an immediate response. Apologizing and sending out a replacement immediately to that subscriber goes a long way toward satisfaction and retention. It's an honest mistake. You did nothing wrong, so don't feel guilty. And a few things like this will not make or break your business. On the contrary, when handled the right way, they can create a deeper connection to those customers and show them how much you care.

Exceptional customer care also means going out of your way to help subscribers navigate your system. If a subscriber needs help updating their credit card because they can't figure out their login, someone from my customer service team hops on the phone with them and helps figure it out. That level of personal attention is huge for my subscribers, especially for those in my older demographic who are not particularly tech-savvy. Instead of them struggling to figure out how to update their information and becoming frustrated, we take on the role of customer concierge and give them the help they need. Those little things make your subscribers feel seen and heard again.

Whether you have 50, 500, or 5,000 subscribers, they all deserve white-glove service. In the beginning, you are the one providing customer care because, let's be honest, you're likely the person doing all the jobs. I know I was, and I would follow up on any questions or issues myself. That became more challenging as my subscription box business grew. The minute that I realized I wasn't answering my customers as quickly as I wanted to, I had to hire someone for that position.

In the beginning, you're the shipper, the marketer, the curator, and the admin. You may even be the accountant and tech support. When you're just getting started, you do it all. I know I did all the jobs, and I probably did all the jobs for far too long. When I started to see that people were upset because I wasn't able to respond to questions and issues quickly enough, I knew I needed to make a change. That's when I hired someone to take over customer care (we'll get into this in more detail in the next chapter). She checked my e-mail boxes, social media comments, direct messages, and more. And she answered questions, handled issues, and provided whatever assistance my subscribers needed quickly and well. My customer service team is still one of the most important parts of my business.

It's nearly certain there will be an issue every month. You won't know what it is going to be, but there is guaranteed to be an issue. When it does happen, take action. Understand what the issue is and decide how you're going to handle it. Remember to put yourself in the place of that buyer. Take off your business-owner hat and don't get caught up in worrying about what fixing the problem is going to cost you. Instead, put yourself in your subscriber's shoes. They've paid money for this subscription, and they allow you to charge their credit card every month. If you've built up trust, they'll come to you ready to give you the opportunity to make it right. Look at it from their lens, and make sure that you handle the situation in the way you would want it to be handled if you were the one with the issue.

When something goes wrong, when a shipment is lost or an item is damaged, you have an opportunity to deepen your relationship with that subscriber. You can turn a negative into a positive and come out of the situation with a lifelong customer who trusts you, because you're the kind of person who cares about them and takes the time to make things right. This is one of the advantages of being small right now. You can offer this concierge customer care. It will go a long way with the people you're serving.

PLAN YOUR NEXT BOX

Here's another point that hopefully goes without saying, but now you get to plan your next box! In Chapter 6 we talked about how to plan out the contents of your first box, so I encourage you to use that 60-second brain dump exercise again. Except this time, try to plan out many months at a time. I run a workshop called "6 in 60," where I teach students to plan six months' worth of subscription boxes in 60 minutes. It's the process I outlined before but in overdrive. Planning your boxes months in advance will save you time and energy not having to do it every month. You can also begin ordering your products further in advance to help alleviate any last-minute stress. And it makes it easier to tease what's in future boxes.

Keep up the good work, friends. Sometimes it takes a few months to get the hang of this and feel like things are really humming along, but it will happen. Soon enough, you'll have to make some big decisions about what's next for you and your business. That's what we'll tackle in the next chapter. Once you're up and running, you can grow as big as you want. It's all up to you. . . .

Action Steps

1. Send out your boxes! Yay!

2. Set a date for your unboxing video.

3. Do the unboxing video and remember to have fun! Follow the seven steps laid out in the chapter.

4. E-mail the link to the unboxing video to all of your subscribers.

5. Brainstorm some social media posts in the next few weeks where you can help your subscribers consume their products.

6. Encourage your subscribers to share and post on social media.

7. Pay close attention to your inbox and respond immediately when a customer has a problem.

8. Plan your next box! You've already done this once, so it should be easier this time. Try planning out a few months' worth of products this time.

Chapter 9

KEEP GOING, KEEP GROWING

One of my favorite Launch Your Box member moments of all time was when Nicole Jenney's GPigBox won the Cube Award for Best Pet Box at SubSummit. SubSummit is the major conference for the subscription box industry—the granddaddy of them all—and the Cube Awards are an enormous deal. Watching one of my members, someone who is super active inside Launch Your Box and who encourages other members and answers all the tech questions all the time, win a huge award filled me with such joy. The fact that she beat out some of the biggest pet boxes in the industry, like BarkBox and BusterBox, made me want to stand on my chair and cheer. I did cheer, loudly, but I kept my feet on the ground.

Nicole spent 15 years working as a graphic designer in the pet space before starting her own pet-supply business, mainly focused on dogs. She found it tough going because the dog space is very crowded. Nicole had always been a pet lover, but when she lost her grandmother, she turned to animals in a new way to comfort her and help her through her grief. It was during that time that she rescued two guinea pigs, Ginny and Pidge. She'd had guinea pigs as a child and Ginny and Pidge reminded her of those happy childhood times. She quickly fell in love with them and had fun spoiling them.

Ginny and Pidge inspired Nicole to focus on small animals, and she quickly found a gap in the market. There were plenty of boxes and subscriptions focused on dogs and cats, but none on guinea pigs. Nicole decided to start a subscription box for guinea pig owners and their pets. Her box provides subscribers with treats, toys, and care products for their pets and fun guinea pig–related items for the owners too.

She completed all the planning steps quickly (she is a tech guru, after all) and launched her box. She already had a business and a passion for guinea pigs, but she didn't have a big audience. On the first day of her launch, she got one subscriber. Nicole describes what happened next as things "blowing up," and within four months, she had 500 subscribers!

Rapid growth demands quick and decisive action, implementing processes and systems, and maintaining outstanding customer service. Nicole maintained focus on providing an excellent subscriber experience as she managed inventory and space challenges. She started fulfilling her subscription boxes from her home but reached the point where she needed to acquire warehouse space to house all the inventory and manage fulfilling hundreds of boxes. She started out as a solopreneur but hired team members as she grew.

The GPigBox isn't just successful and exciting on its own. It has also brought new attention, more sales, and exciting opportunities to Nicole's larger business. And it all started with Ginny and Pidge, who brought Nicole some much needed comfort in a dark time.

Nicole's win that day wasn't just a big moment for her, it was a big moment for all of us inside Launch Your Box. So many of our members were there, taking advantage of the networking and learning opportunities SubSummit provides. We had so much fun being together and turning online biz besties into real-life friendships! The energy we all received from being together was incredible. As a matter of fact, a lot of people asked who we were and how they could join us. Our energy was contagious, and the fun we had was visible to everyone. We cheer each other on constantly, and that was magnified in real life.

YOU ARE A CEO NOW

Nicole is the CEO of her business. It was when she leaned in to that title, stepped up to the plate, and started making some big decisions that she was able to win such a huge award. You have officially launched a business, which officially makes you a CEO too. Do you think of yourself that way? I know it can be hard to step into that role, but owning it is powerful. You get to be the owner of a successful subscription box business by seeing and seeking out opportunities. Every day you work hard, face challenges, solve problems, get creative, and take risks. In other words, what CEOs do on a daily basis.

So much of being an entrepreneur depends on personal growth. As you grow in your role, your business grows stronger. Approaching challenges with the energy and mindset of a CEO requires a vision of the long-term outcome, not just a short-term get-it-done attitude. As your business grows, settle into your role as the CEO. Thinking of yourself as the CEO of your business makes a difference. I believe 75 percent of being an entrepreneur is mindset.

It's that important. A fear-filled scarcity mindset limits you and holds you back from being the CEO in your company. Replace that fear with a sense of abundance and gratitude and it will change everything you do in your business.

You've launched your box, and whether you've been in this for one month or one year, you know you have a proven concept. You have subscribers, you have processes, you've figured out the back end. Growth requires change, and being an effective CEO means being willing to make those changes to build a strong, sustainable subscription box business that will serve your business and your life for years to come. This takes time. Sometimes people do launch with a bang, and their business takes off faster than they expected. But generally it grows gradually. And I think that's good. Slow, controlled growth is better in the beginning. It gives you time to establish systems and processes that will support your business as it grows. It allows you to maintain excellent customer service and provide an outstanding subscriber experience. Once you've gotten all that in place, if continued growth is your goal, it's time to put a little gas on that fire. In this chapter, we'll examine the different parts of your business you'll need to focus on as you grow.

FROM BOOTSTRAPPING TO TEAM BUILDING

I hired my first person before I added a subscription box to my business. I had received a local order for 60 hand-painted items and thought I could handle it. I thought I'd just work late, work some extra hours, and it would all be fine. Well, as my deadline drew closer and closer, I knew I wasn't going to make it. I talked my friends into helping me and paid them with beer and pizza. They helped me get all the things painted, and fortunately we did hit our deadline. They did the base coats, and I did the finishing touches. At some point during the whirlwind, my friend Amber looked at me and said, "You really, really need to hire someone. I don't mind helping you anytime you need it. But you're not slowing down."

I knew she was right. I just needed someone to tell it to me straight. I had resisted it for so long, and I wasn't even giving myself a regular paycheck at that time. How was I now going to pay someone else when I wasn't even paying myself? But I did it. I hired someone just to help me through the month of December. The Christmas orders were killing me, so I told her I would hire her just for the Christmas season. Eight years later, she still works for me.

After I hired that first employee, I was almost instantly able to give myself a regular paycheck. It was incredible what she did for my business. I thought having her there meant I would be able to double my output. Instead, I more than quadrupled my output, because we were so efficient. We streamlined processes. She would prep the things, I would finish them, and she would prep more. I had to keep working because she was right behind me. Having her there freed me up and greatly increased my productivity. She could help customers in the store and answer the phone. I could stay focused on whatever I needed to be doing, the things only I could do. Hiring her really helped me—and really helped my business.

It wasn't until I started the subscription box that I hired my next person. I thought, *If I'm going to do this, I'm going to need even more help.* That's when I decided to hire my assistant. She checked my inbox and answered the direct messages on my social media pages. I hired her for admin help, and she became my extra set of hands, ready to jump in and help wherever I needed her.

These first two hires are typically the first ones a sub-scription box owner makes: a virtual assistant (VA) to handle admin stuff and someone who can take care of some of the things that you "normally do." Before I hired my assistant, I was doing so many tasks; I call them $10-an-hour jobs. I was packing up everything. I was printing out the shipping labels. I was changing people's sizes on the website. And at the end of the day, I was so exhausted from all the tasks, I didn't have time or the creative energy to plan out next month's box or design a new T-shirt, which are not only the things I love doing but also the things I'm great at.

I didn't have enough bandwidth to think ahead because I was trying to get the daily activities done.

It took time to let go. First I *kind of* let go of the shipping, then I *kind of* let go of all the messages, and then finally I *kind of* let go of the customer service role. It was a gradual process, and even when I "let go," it still took me a little time to fully let go. But every time I delegated something, it freed up my brain to think more about the next collection I was going to curate. And it finally allowed me to get ahead of the planning for the boxes. I had been planning month to month (this might still be you). I didn't have enough bandwidth to think ahead because I was trying to get the daily activities done. So by removing all these tasks from me, I was now able to think more creatively. I was able to take more of a big-picture look at the business and get ahead of things instead of reacting all the time.

Now we're a team of 16, and every hire took something off my plate. That's really the important point to understand here. I couldn't grow and scale the way I did if I still performed all these jobs. If you're still in month one of your business, I know thinking of hiring and scaling sounds like it might be far off, and maybe even scary. But it's likely closer than you think. Considering how to grow through hiring, even at such an early stage, can set you up for success.

> *Spend more time working on your business instead of in your business.*

GROWING YOUR TEAM

As you scale your subscription box business, it won't be possible to do it all yourself. You will need a team. Attracting, hiring, and developing the right people in the right roles can make your life easier. Your business will grow faster, you'll spend more time working *on* your business instead of *in* your business, and you'll even be able to spend less time working.

Where Can You Find Good People?

Let's say you've decided you need a team in order to continue to grow. How do you find the right people for these preliminary roles? Here are some of my top tips:

1. **Get referrals from other business owners.** A word-of-mouth recommendation is always the best way to go. Nothing is worth more than an endorsement from someone you trust.

2. **Find freelance specialists or project managers on online marketplaces.** There are many places online to find good help; it just

may take a little searching and filtering. Sites like Upwork, Fiverr, and Storetasker are great for hiring a VA or someone for a specific task on a project. You can find more resources for this on SarahsBookBonus.com.

3. **Hire VAs or other key roles through educational programs.** In the past, to hire for my business I have partnered with service-based coaches who train people in specific roles. You can learn more about the resources I use for this at SarahsBookBonus.com.

Be Ready to Lead, Teach, and Train

Just like you are looking for great team members, people are looking for great places to work. It's up to you to provide team members with what they need to be successful. If you want to be a good CEO, I recommend you do the following:

- Provide a good work environment.
- Give your team members structure to do their jobs well.
- Lead, teach, and train your team.

Remember, your employees are not an expense, they are an investment.

Independent Contractors vs. W-2 Employees

Each time you add a member to your team, you need to decide whether they will be a full- or part-time employee or an independent contractor. There are clear differences between employees and independent contractors, and it's important you understand those differences. I have both on my team for the different needs of different roles.

In simple terms, independent contractors:

- Are self-employed. They work for themselves and are not technically employed by you.
- Supply their own work tools
- Submit invoices for their work. You do not take taxes out of the payment.
- Typically work for more clients than just you
- Work on whatever projects you assign, but you don't have control over how they complete their work

Examples of independent contractors subscription box owners use:

- Web developers
- Graphic designers
- Community or social media managers
- Freelance writers or copywriters
- Sourcing agents

In simple terms, employees:

- Work at your location or work remotely using your equipment
- Have earnings that are subject to payroll taxes such as FICA and income tax withholding
- Only work for you (typically)
- Are managed by you, both in terms of the work they do and how they complete it

Set Up Your Team for Success

Even if you only have one team member other than your-self, you need to set them up for success and act like a CEO. Following you'll find some principles I use to make sure my team is ready from day one:

1. **Outline and define their roles.** You cannot set a team member up for success if they don't know what their role is. Make sure that everyone on your team understands exactly what their job requirements are and what tasks they own.

2. **Identify their strengths.** Identify the gifts, skills, or talents each team member brings and help work them into those areas of your business. Your business will greatly benefit by letting your team lean in to their strengths.

3. **Communicate regularly.** There is no way to have a cohesive team without constant communication.

4. **Give them decision-making power.** Team members take greater ownership of a task or role when they are able to contribute to decisions. Your team members are collaborators and want agency. Everyone likes to feel like they have some power and control and aren't micromanaged.

5. **Set and give goals.** Give team members something to work toward. Share your vision so it becomes their vision too. People work hard and care about what they're doing when their work means something.

Common Excuses for Not Hiring

I talk to people all the time in my membership about hiring: when to hire, who to hire, why to hire, and so on. My general opinion is that people almost always wait too long. If you're debating whether it's time to hire, it almost certainly is. But there are always things holding people back. Here are some of the most common reasons I hear from people for not hiring (when they almost certainly need to):

- **"I don't have the money."** Ask yourself how many subscribers you need to add in order to pay for that person. Do a little subscription box math. I bet you could hit that number if you need to.

- **"No one wants to work."** Take the time to hire the right people and create a great working environment and watch your amazing team build. People do want to work; you just need to hire carefully and believe in them.

- **"It takes too much time to train people."** Let's flip this. You don't have time not to hire someone. Remember how my business exploded when I made some strategic hires? It sounds a little backward, but as your productivity increases as you build your team, so will your income.

- **"I need to be more organized before I hire someone."** Make your first hire someone who can help you with organization and streamlining processes. Don't wait until you have it all together or you'll never do it. Let people in on the messy middle of business.

As the CEO of your business, you need to build a team to support you and your business as you scale. Take the time to hire well, onboard with care, and provide your team members with the opportunity to succeed in their positions and grow into new roles.

A member of my community (Launch Your Box and Scale Your Box), Cheryl, has a subscription box of yarn for avid knitting enthusiasts. She hand-dyes all her yarn, and at a certain point in her business, she absolutely could not dye any more yarn herself. She was out of room and out of hands. Hiring and investing in more space felt scary. The demand was there, her audience and subscriptions were only growing, but she couldn't keep up. Eventually she invested in renting a warehouse for space, hired a few people to do the dyeing, and watched her box business explode. This is the power of letting go, allowing people to help, and trusting that you can figure out the rest. Often the only way to grow is to spend some money and hire help. I guarantee you'll recoup your investment.

UNDERSTAND YOUR BUYING POWER

After you've been running your box for a few months and seen consistent growth, it's worth examining how you can save money on purchasing and deepen relationships with vendors. I work with a lot of vendors and manufacturers sourcing products for my subscription box. I have vendors I've bought from for years, building relationships and negotiating better prices and terms, as my buying power has grown. I am confident negotiating with them. They know and like me, and I know and like them. I appreciate the quality of their goods, and they value me and the revenue I bring to their businesses. So when I had the opportunity to work directly with the licensing company for Kate Spade to design some custom products for my boxes, you'd think I would have taken that same confidence to those meetings.

But that's not what happened. My old enemy, self-doubt, reared its ugly head. Somewhere along the way, maybe during my flight, I forgot how hard I'd worked to establish myself and my business in the subscription box industry. I forgot that purchasing thousands of pieces from a vendor or manufacturer meant that I had clout; I had buying power. I forgot all of that and instead let my head fill with all the thoughts of how small and insignificant my business probably was to them.

Maybe it was the fact that I'd loved this brand and all it represented for years. Maybe it seemed more "big time" than I imagined I was ready for. No matter the reason, I walked into that meeting feeling small. The good news is that the Kate Spade people couldn't see my self-doubt. They had no idea what I was feeling, and maybe I was even good at faking it. What they saw was a business owner who wanted to order thousands of items from them and enter into an ongoing relationship that would bring them a lot of revenue. Once I realized how much they wanted to work with me, I settled down, remembered who I was and why I deserved to be there, and even had some fun.

As your subscription box business and your subscriber numbers grow, so does your buying power. When you're buying hundreds or thousands of items at a time, your negotiating power with vendors and manufacturers is much greater than during the early days when you might only need 25 of something. The higher your numbers grow, the more buying power you have.

When you develop a relationship with a vendor and purchase from them month after month, you become a source of recurring revenue for them. That gives you power and also makes the relationship mutually beneficial.

Who Do You Have Buying Power With?

Your buying power isn't limited to vendors you purchase products from. Think about all the other things you purchase for your subscriptions month after month. You buy from:

- Packaging suppliers
- Printers
- Product vendors

Consider what getting your bulk business every month means to a vendor. Then consider what you can negotiate from them. Here are a few ideas:

- A regular discount
- Free shipping
- Extra pieces in your shipment
- Show specials or closeout items
- Payment terms

Here's a little exercise to get your ideas flowing. Choose an item you regularly put in your subscription box. Spend time calculating potential savings with various types of discounts or perks to help you decide where to start with your negotiations.

If there are vendors you already have strong relationships with, start with them. Then look for other vendors with whom you can make connections. Understanding your buying power and working with your vendors can increase your monthly profits. Plus it just feels great. When you make your first negotiation, you will feel like such a boss. Understand the power you have and use it.

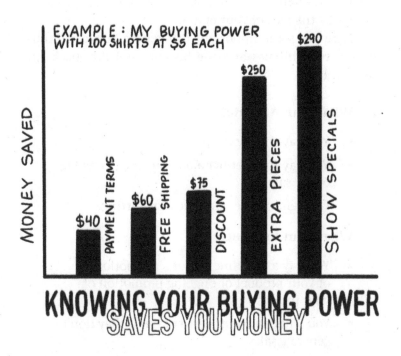

GROWING WITH AFFILIATES AND INFLUENCERS

You know how important it is to get in front of new people—to build your audience and get more traffic. What if you didn't have to do all that audience building yourself? You can tap into other people's audiences, and they can get some traffic to your website without you having to find all those people yourself. This is called affiliate and influencer marketing. If you're on social media, you likely see this all the time already. I know in Chapter 1 I said I am the influencer of my business, and so are you, by the way. But it's still a great strategy to tap into the audience of other influencers, as long as you remember that you'll always be the face of your brand.

Here are some important differences between influencers and affiliates and the benefits and drawbacks to using each:

What Is an Affiliate?

- You pay the person per sale.
- You pay them either a flat rate or a percentage of the sale.
- Payment can be one time or recurring.

What Is an Influencer?

- You pay a one-time fee for a promotion of your product or ongoing promotion of your product.
- You still pay an influencer even if they don't generate sales.
- Influencers are used more for brand awareness and brand reputation.

I prefer affiliate marketing. It's a win-win for you and the affiliate. They don't make money unless I make money. It's better for your business because the affiliate has more incentive to promote and re-promote your subscription box. The revenue they generate is directly tied to how many subscribers they get for you.

Paying an Affiliate

The industry average for an affiliate is 5 to 20 percent per sale, but it's ultimately up to you how much you offer your affiliates. You can also offer a flat-rate commission, like $5 to $10 per box. Carefully consider what you can afford to give, and always keep your profit margin in mind. Remember, you are in business to make a profit. Protect your profit margin (at least 30 percent).

Your goal is to create a commission that works for you but also gives the affiliate a reason to promote your subscription box. Realize that if you don't make it worth their time, they won't promote you.

Finding Affiliates and Influencers

Anyone who has an audience is an influencer. When considering who to ask to be an affiliate or influencer for your box, think about your own subscribers who own a business or run a social media group. They might be great affiliates for you. After all, you already know they love what you're selling. The easiest place to start is whoever you already follow or is in your network. If you've crossed paths a few times, chances are that you'll be a natural fit.

When searching social media for possible affiliates or influencers that you don't yet know, search niche-specific keywords. Make sure anyone you consider aligns with your values and mission. They will be representing you and your brand.

As in all parts of your business, when it comes to working with affiliates and influencers, relationships matter. Build a relationship first. E-mailing or messaging them with the ask as your first interaction usually isn't a great plan. Read their blog, follow them on social media, engage with their content, and get to know them a little. Coming on strong at the beginning makes people feel like you're just trying to increase sales. You can look to promote your business and also care about them and the relationship. Just treat them like a normal human and be authentic. Establish that mutual "know, like, and trust," and be sincere in all communications.

I have affiliates for my subscription box. They are subscribers who have audiences that are my ideal customers. My affiliates do box openings on their social media channels, and they get affiliate commissions. I pay a lot of money every month to my affiliates, but again, they only make that money when people subscribe.

FILLING YOUR FUNNEL

Your funnel is the gateway people take to becoming a subscriber. Parts of your funnel can be social media, different segments of your e-mail list, different subscriber tiers, and so on. It doesn't matter how many subscribers you have or how much monthly recurring revenue your subscription box is bringing in. You never stop audience building. You will have members cancel. That's completely normal and there are many reasons for it, but the most important point to remember is that it's almost never personal. Wish them well and inform your list that you're opening up more spots. Filling those spots and continuing to grow by gaining more subscribers, building your audience, and funneling people to your waitlist is a must.

To constantly drive people to your waitlist to fill the top of your funnel, you need a multichannel marketing plan. Each part of your marketing plan requires you to plan and create consistent content. Here's what I recommend for each part.

You never stop audience building.

Your E-mail Marketing Plan

You already know how important e-mail is; we've covered that thoroughly. You cannot rely on social media alone to be seen. E-mail marketing is alive and well and needs to be part of your overall marketing plan beyond just your launches and initial business start-up. Revenue from e-mail marketing should be more than 20 percent of your sales; that's a general marker for how you know your efforts are working. If you don't have an e-mail marketing plan yet, it's time to create one. You're leaving money on the table.

Weekly E-mails

It's easy to know what to say when you're in the middle of a launch or hyping your soon-to-be subscription box. It's much harder when you're an established business and need to come up with content regularly. But still, you need to e-mail your list each week. It's important to stay on people's minds and not be a stranger. These e-mails should be short, sweet, and highly visual. Hook your reader and tell them what you want to tell them clearly and concisely.

Almost every day, someone inside Launch Your Box will ask, "What do I say?" when talking about e-mail marketing. The great thing is you don't have to create brand-new content for these e-mails. Instead, pull from all the content you're already creating. Some of the weekly e-mails I send out include:

1. Repurposing a weekly live video into an e-mail

2. Box openings

3. Special promotions

4. Favorite items of the week

5. Five ways to use an item from the monthly box

6. Something personal—a cool story from a subscriber, a story about my week, and so on

Your SMS/Text Marketing Plan

Texts have become a large part of any e-commerce marketing plan. If you're not already using SMS/text marketing, now is the time to start.

- Nearly 100 percent of text messages are seen—*a lot* more than e-mails or social posts.

- It's not "one more thing"—you're already doing the things.

- SMS/text marketing simply drives traffic to your posts, lives, videos, and so on.

Use SMS/text marketing strategically and avoid spamming your list. This means no daily texting. Choose a couple things each week to text your list about, and make sure you have a goal for each text. Your goals should be to engage, make connections, and ask for the sale.

6 Strategies for SMS/Text Marketing

1. Invite them to a live.
2. Give first access to that month's box, a new item, and so on.
3. Discounts or sales.
4. Subscriber shares.
5. Create a box waitlist.
6. Sneak peeks.

Paid Ads

Paid ads can work great, but they are not a magic button you can press to get people to subscribe. You cannot simply throw some money at running an ad and expect it to work. This cannot be your only marketing plan. Paid ads can be a great way to boost engagement, drive traffic, and generate sales, but they are not a magical way to instantly grow your subscriber numbers. Before you dive into paid ads, make sure you have developed a strong multichannel marketing strategy using what you learned in earlier sections of this chapter.

When you are ready to make paid ads part of your marketing strategy, the first question you'll have is: How much should I spend on advertising? E-commerce industry standards are 5 to 10 percent of your gross revenue. But that does not mean you *need* to spend that much. You should figure out what you're comfortable spending. My general advice is:

- Make sure you've dialed in organic traffic first! If you do not have regular organic traffic, you are not ready to start paying for it.

- Set a budget and stick with it. It is very easy for ads to eat into your profits.

- Allocate your ads budget to three areas:
  - Promotions
  - Audience building
  - Retargeting

- Use your most engaging posts for ads.

- Don't be afraid to boost.

- Give it time.
  - Give it a week before deciding whether an ad is working.
  - If the ad is performing well, up the budget 20 percent every three to four days.

Growing your business comes with its challenges, but it's exciting and can be so much fun. The strategies I've laid out in this chapter will help you with the practicalities, but remember, the biggest key is your mindset. Know that you can do this. Remember that hang-ups and setbacks are normal—and you are capable of figuring them out. That is the CEO's mindset. You are in charge of your business and your future and can make this thing whatever you want it to be. Take it one step at a time. You're just getting started. . . .

Know that you can do this.

Action Steps

1. Call yourself a CEO. This might seem silly, but identifying yourself that way is the first step in owning it.

2. Make a list of some tasks you'd like taken off your plate. What do you do that anyone can do? What can only you do? Think of how to free up your time to focus on those income-producing activities that belong to only you.

3. If you're ready to hire, identify the first role you'd like to fill. Maybe it's a virtual assistant or an in-person assistant to help pack and ship.

4. Take some time to define and outline that role. This will help you hire and instruct that person.

5. Consider one product where you might negotiate a better price with a vendor.

6. Research affiliates and influencers and decide on one place to start. Maybe with just one affiliate or one influencer. Dip your toe in and see what happens.

7. Create your multichannel marketing plan. Don't get into ads until you're sure your organic traffic is on point.

Chapter 10

CREATE YOUR OWN PATH

I'm a big believer in coaching. I have a life coach and a business coach. I've coached thousands of people on how to start, launch, and grow a subscription box business. I've got coaching down, and I can spot the one thing that's holding someone back in their business. I can trouble-shoot messaging that's not working, suggest small or big tweaks to social media marketing efforts, and give tough love when it means the difference between a profitable business that sustains you and an expensive hobby. I've had business coaches and mentors, people I've learned from and continue to learn from as I grow both sides of my business. So, it was easy for me to recognize one day that I needed some help when I found myself stressed and overwhelmed, trying to juggle all the things in my life.

When I meet with my coach, I do most of the talking. He asks questions and I talk; that's a hallmark sign of a great coach—they lead you to find the answers and make the conclusions on your own. Almost always there's a light-bulb moment or a realization. One week, I had a lot going on and my stress level was high. My coach and I had a conversation about what I needed to get off my plate. And he asked, "Do you think it's time you hired a designer?"

My response came quickly and from my soul. "If I hire a designer, that takes away the only job I have left that I love." The thought of not designing took my breath away. If I hired a designer, if someone else created the inspirational T-shirts I'm known for, then I'd feel like I was just pushing paper. It wasn't the lightbulb moment I expected, but it was the one I needed. Even after all these years, I'm still creating my own path and discovering what that looks like.

I didn't want to grow to the point where I could no longer do the part of my job I truly love. I want to be the designer in my business. I remember talking to Stu McLaren years before when he was interviewing me for a spot in his mastermind. At that time, I was doing all the jobs inside of my subscription box business. He asked me what I wanted to be in my business in five years, and I replied: I would love to just be the designer. I would love to be the curator, designing all the products and having someone else make and pack them. And now, sitting and talking with my coach, I realized that I'd reached that point where if my business grew much bigger I wouldn't have time to design anymore. The part of my business that I love more than anything was the part I was beginning to not have time for. It was a red flag. That was my signal that I needed to take a step back and make some adjustments.

IT'S YOUR BUSINESS; IT'S YOUR PATH

One of the incredible aspects of being a subscription box owner is that you get to build a business that serves you. With hard work and dedication to serving your audience, you have the opportunity to decide how large you want your business to be. And, like me, you have the privilege of deciding when big enough is, in fact, big enough. I know wildly successful subscription box owners with businesses of all shapes and sizes. Their success is not determined by the number of subscribers they have or the amount of revenue they bring in. Rather, it has everything to do with what their businesses make possible in their lives.

This is *your path,* and this journey is about making your business what you want it to be in a way that serves you. If you're only in your first month of business, right now I want you to focus on getting this subscription box business of yours off the ground. It's okay to not know what you want this business to be just yet. You're starting your business and might be doing everything you can just to make sales. That's your focus, and rightly so. You need to sell products, plain and simple. And it's not until you start selling products and start making some money that you start to think, *Okay, now what do I want?* (By the way, you might be a visionary and already know *exactly* what you want, and that is fantastic too. Keep that vision in mind.)

> *This journey is about making your business what you want it to be in a way that serves you.*

You probably have something that drew you to this business. Maybe it's making some extra money or, like me, wanting to do work that you love. Most of the time, the first thing you want is a steady paycheck. And then you soon realize that a close second is the freedom of not worrying about the bills in your business. Not until those two things happen can you even consider things like wanting more time to yourself. You are so busy, hustling just to make the money that will replace an income from a job you quit or you're still waiting to quit. Later, you'll have choices. You'll be able to say, "Oh, I don't have to do everything. I don't have to work all the time. I can choose time over money." That time is coming, I promise. Just keep following the strategies in this book and you'll get there.

WHAT DO YOU WANT NOW?

Once you do get things off the ground, and you're making sales and things are chugging along, you can breathe a little, take a step back, and analyze what you want your subscription box business to look like in terms of your actual life. You can then answer the question: What do I want now? You've hustled and worked your face off. You've implemented all the processes. You've tackled the tech and won! You've had weeks where you used an entire bottle of dry shampoo on your hair because you really didn't have time to wash it. You've done all the things. You probably didn't even know why you were doing some of them. It was a lot of hard work. But now you've built this business. Now it's time to ask yourself what it is you want from the business you've worked so hard to create.

No one can answer that question for you. You may want to keep pushing, keep growing, and see just how far you can take your subscription box business. Or you may decide that right where you are is the perfect spot to spend some time, focusing on nurturing and retaining your subscribers and improving systems and processes to bring greater ease. Your "What do I want now?" might be somewhere in the middle, focused on slow, steady growth that feels manageable. *Again, there is no right answer to this question. There is only the right answer for you.* Keep your why firmly in mind and run opportunities and decisions through the filter of, "Does this support what I want for my business and my life?" Remember why you started. What drove you to this business in the first place?

One important aspect to consider is knowing what part of this business you love doing the most. I know I want to be the designer—I always have and always will. And the red line in my business is that I'll never grow so big that I can't play that role anymore. Do you have something like that in your business? I have found among my students that their answers are often similar: they love picking out products or designing. That seems to be a main reason why we've picked this business. But if during your entrepreneurial path you discovered you love something else about the CEO role, that's great too. The important thing is that you figure out what you love and make sure you can keep doing it. That's what will keep this business fun and sustainable for you.

You get to decide what this business is and how big it gets. You get to decide whether you're going to manage a warehouse and employees or keep it small and manageable on your own. I mentioned my fellow subscription box business owners who have much larger businesses than mine with many more subscribers. I made the decision to control the growth of my subscriptions in order to stay in alignment with the life I want for myself, my family, and my employees.

When I opened my brick-and-mortar store, I was a one-woman show. If I needed to run to the bank, I had to close the store for half an hour. If I had a meeting at school or wanted to go watch one of my kids in a performance or one of them had a doctor's appointment, I had to close the store for part of the day. If I wasn't there, no sales were happening. I couldn't be there for all of my kids' special events and was missing soccer games and band performances and dinners with my family. Of course, that wasn't okay with me.

By the time I started my subscription box, I had hired someone to work part time in my shop. But I had added all the work that went along with launching and growing a subscription box business. I was still working too many hours. I was still missing things that were important to me. I had a small team helping me, but there were still hours to cover at the store, as well as all the work that went into packing and shipping boxes every month. If someone was sick or not able to come to work, I had to step in for them. I was the business owner and the buck stopped with me.

WHEN EVERYTHING CHANGED, I REALIZED MY BUSINESS COULD TOO

It took a worldwide crisis to show me things could be different. When the pandemic hit in 2020, my world changed overnight just like everyone else's. As a nonessential business, my store was shut down, and I didn't know how long that closure would last. My team and I weren't allowed to work in the store prepping and packing the subscription boxes. I worried whether my business could survive or if this was going to be the end of all of my hard work.

I quickly pivoted and moved all of my inventory online, adding so many products to what had been a very small online store. With everyone home, my online store took off. I spent a lot of time live on social media, connecting with my audience. Not selling, but simply serving them by being there. We were all scared and craving connection. They already trusted me and knew my content and brand, which meant they were happy to spend time with me online. They were also excited to buy from my online store.

We had to get scrappy to continue shipping out our subscription boxes. My team showed up big for me, taking inventory home and prepping and packing boxes from their kitchens, living rooms, and spare rooms. I needed that subscription box revenue to pay the bills for my business and to pay my employees while they had to stay home. My store was only closed for 45 days, but those days taught me a lot. They showed me the power of having an online store and how successful we could be without having a physical location for people to shop. They showed me how valuable my subscription box was to my overall business security and success. And they showed me how much I valued having more time away from my business and more time with my family.

When I saw the possibility of having this business without the brick-and-mortar store, I was excited. I decided to close the retail store and move into a large warehouse space ideally suited for all the things we needed to make the subscription box side of the business run as smoothly and efficiently as possible. We kept one small area at the front of the space for customers to come in and shop, but during limited hours. The best part was that I was able to design a work schedule around my needs and the needs of my team. We're all moms of school-age kids. That meant we all had carpool drop-off and pickup responsibilities as well as kids' activities and special events to manage and attend. Creating a work schedule that begins after school starts in the morning and ends by three in the afternoon means I can provide well-paying, flexible jobs for an amazing group of moms who can still be there for their families just like I can be for mine. This is what my ideal business looks like. Yours may be different.

I dreamed of building a business that reflected my love for creativity and fun and trendy fashions and accessories that also supported my family. I'm proud to say I've done that. I worked hard and made my dream come true. And when I have a new idea—which happens multiple times a day—I run it through that filter of whether trying that new thing or adding that new option would continue to serve my goals. If it doesn't, it can wait. No amount of money is worth sacrificing the life I've designed for myself and my employees.

SUBSCRIPTION BOX MATH

During the early months of my subscription box, when I was still in the active growth phase, I used subscription box math whenever there was something new I needed to buy or pay for. This is a half-joke but also entirely serious idea my students and I talk about in my membership. Subscription box math is, basically, when you want something, you calculate how many boxes you need to sell to get it. One time, we wanted to plan a family trip to Costa Rica. It was expensive, completely outside my pay scale at that point in my business. I could have just decided that the trip wasn't going to happen. I could have put that dream trip aside, into the "maybe next year" slot. Instead, I used some subscription box math. If the trip cost a certain amount of money and we planned to travel in six months, I calculated how many new subscribers I needed in order to cover the cost of the trip. That number turned out to be 50. If I got 50 new subscribers and saved for six months, we would have the money to take that trip to Costa Rica. That's subscription box math.

My daughter is a talented athlete. She wanted to start playing club soccer, which comes with a big commitment of players' time and a large financial commitment from families. She works so hard and loves playing soccer so much, I was desperate to give her every possible opportunity to succeed. I'm sure all the parents out there can identify with that. It was time to figure out what I needed to do to cover the additional cost. My subscription box math that time turned out to be an additional 10 subscribers a month. You better believe I went out and made it happen. Nothing is a stronger motivator than your children.

As my business grew and regular everyday family and home expenses and special things we wanted to do as a family came up, I turned to subscription box math over and over. When I needed a new car, I calculated how many additional subscribers I needed in order to cover the car payment. My subscription business grew based on the needs that grew with it. That was motivation to say, all right, let's go get some new subscribers, Mama's getting a new car. For every new expense I asked, "How many more subscribers do I need to be able to afford that?" And that's how I operated for a long time. *We're going to go on vacation. All right, let's go get 50 new subscribers.*

I don't have to do subscription box math anymore. We have enough money coming in regularly that whatever we need, I know we can afford it. I'm sure your subscription box math looks different than mine, but the point is the same. That's the beauty of being an entrepreneur: we have the power to make money when we want to. If your family needs something, you have a lever to pull and make it happen. People working in nine-to-five jobs don't have that.

They're working with a finite salary and need to budget within that amount. With subscription boxes, there are no limits on revenue. If you understand your ideal customer and what they want, if you build an audience of engaged followers, and if you deliver an outstanding experience, the sky's the limit.

Each step along the way, as you consider growing your business by adding subscribers to make your subscription box math work, check in with yourself. Ask yourself if that growth aligns with the life you're trying to create. If growth starts to feel stressful or overwhelming, if it's taking away from the life and business you want to create, you can slow down. How much you promote and launch is completely within your control. And I always remind people that if you get underwater, you can always hire help. It's amazing what one right person in your business can do for you instead of having to scale back. You can get to a point of stability where you're not measuring things based on the additional number of boxes you'd need to sell. I got there. And that's a beautiful place to be.

If you're someone who wants to go for it, to see just how far you can take your subscription box business, you can do that. I have friends who have tens of thousands of subscribers, who have large teams working in their businesses to support them, and who manage multiple distribution locations. And for them, that is incredible. They have built large businesses that allow them to live very comfortable lives and seek big things for their businesses. I'm sure some of you achievers out there reading this have a goal to get as big as you can. I support that.

For me, I know I don't need to have 50,000 subscribers to have the business and life I want. I don't need a $30 million business to be successful. I am successful and know that however many subscribers I have doesn't make or break who I am or how great my business is. I have a friend who has 28,000 subscribers and is in awe of how much profit I have compared to his business. I know I don't have to have a 100-person staff or 28,000 subscribers to make a lot of money. That's the business I've intentionally chosen.

SURROUND YOURSELF WITH LIKE-MINDED PEOPLE

Now is the right time to tell you something that might come as a surprise, but it's important for you to know. Not everyone in your life wants to talk to you about your subscription box every day. I know, it's shocking—it's so fun to talk about! How could anyone not want to?! But it's true. I used to bore my family to death talking about the idea for my subscription box, all the things I still needed to figure out (tech!), and how much I just knew my subscribers would love my box. The truth was they just didn't care that much. Not because they're not supportive; they totally are. This industry—this fun, exciting world of subscription boxes—is my world, not theirs. My friends don't want to hear about my business every time we meet for lunch or coffee or when we're sitting in the stands or on the sidelines, watching our kids play sports. If I only talk to them about my subscription box and what's going on in my business, they'll stop inviting me to lunch and start pretending not to see me at games. That's certainly not what I want.

But this doesn't mean you don't need people to share your business life with. You absolutely do. The life of an entrepreneur can be really lonely, especially during the early days when it's just you. You need to spend some time with like-minded people, other business owners who can relate to the challenges and opportunities that arise with this type of business. You owe it to yourself to find a community of people who will support and encourage you and for whom you can do the same.

I have a close-knit group of women I call my "biz besties." None of our businesses are exactly the same, but we get along great and all have the same goal of supporting our families and creating lives we love. They are all busy moms, juggling successful businesses and families. They are generous with their time and are always willing to hash out problems I'm trying to solve or talk through new ideas. Honestly, I would be lost without them. These women have been integral to helping me create my own path in entrepreneurship. They know me and my goals. When I throw them an idea at midnight on a Saturday, they can help me sort through whether that aligns with what I'm trying to do or is just a fun, one-off thing that better wait. They keep me in check. Sometimes, others are better at seeing things clearly about us than we are. I encourage you to find your own group of supportive business owners who can help you create your own path and provide answers when things are murky. Inside Launch Your Box, so many of my members have found biz besties in each other. Many of these women have never met, but their friendships are as strong as their businesses. They get one another in a way that other people in their lives simply can't.

Joining a Mastermind

There comes a time, after you've made it through the early stages of your subscription box business and you're ready to start growing and exploring the possibilities of your business, when you might be ready for something a little more formal than business friends. When I reached that point, I knew I had hit a ceiling and needed to learn more and grow as a business owner, so I decided to join a mastermind. A mastermind is led by someone who acts as the organizer and facilitator, usually someone at least a few steps ahead of where the participants are in their businesses. This is still a group of like-minded people, like my besties, but this group has a definite structure to it and specific objectives.

When I decided a mastermind was the logical next step in my development as a business owner, I wasn't even sure exactly what happened inside of one. I had heard of masterminds and knew all the big names in my industry were involved, so I thought it must be the thing to do. I researched different masterminds that were connected in some way to people I knew through my business. They were people I had taken a course from or learned from in a different way, or even just people whose business journeys I had watched.

Pretty soon I discovered that I couldn't just join a mastermind—I had to apply and be accepted. So I applied to my first mastermind and . . . I got denied. It was a blow to my ego and made me think, *Well, maybe I'm not good enough to be in a mastermind; maybe I'm not there yet.* At that time, I had a pretty solid business, but I didn't have thousands of subscribers. I knew I might not be the most successful person in these groups, but I did still believe I had something to offer. Something inside me told me to keep trying. So I applied for another mastermind. I was the most nervous about this one because it was almost triple the cost of the first mastermind, the one that rejected me. I did my subscription box math to calculate how many subscribers I needed to have to join and got to work marketing. After I applied, I didn't hear anything for a month. I assumed that meant I wasn't good enough to be in that mastermind either. Self-doubt came rushing back, along with negative self-talk. I mean, why did I think I was good enough for that mastermind when I wasn't good enough for the first one?

I decided to just let go of the idea of a mastermind for the time being. And then I received a call. It was the day before Christmas Eve and the call was from Stu McLaren, who you know by now because I've mentioned him a few times (plus he wrote the Foreword for you Foreword-skippers). He ran the mastermind that was triple the cost. By then, I had almost changed my mind. The *I'm not even making enough money yet. Who do I think I am?* thoughts came again. I had decided I needed to just stay focused on my business and grow it alone. But Stu called and said, "I got your application for the mastermind. I want to talk about it."

After I got done freaking out for a few minutes, he started asking me questions. He wanted to know where I saw my business in the next five years, and I already told you the answer. It's the same now as it was then: I want to be the curator, the designer. "I don't want to be the packer or the laborer anymore," I told him. Stu and I had a conversation, and the next day he invited me to join the mastermind. It wasn't totally smooth sailing after that, as you know from Chapter 1. But that mastermind changed my life and the life of my business. I'm so glad I followed through and decided to join.

Whether it's with a group of biz besties or inside a mastermind, it's important to have a safe place where there's room for the personal and the business. So much of business *is* personal, and it's okay to let it be that. You pour your heart and soul into creating a business, so of course it's personal. Inside a mastermind, you're able to dial in your business and talk about tactics and strategies you've never thought about before. But you also get to know those people on a personal level.

There is no one path to subscription box success.

After I'd been in a few masterminds and teaching in others for a while, it occurred to me to create that type of environment for my own people, for my own members who want to keep working through the hard things together. I created my own mastermind, and it's a joy— and one of the best things I get to do.

There is no one path to subscription box success. It's your business and your why. You get to decide how big is big enough. Those friends I just mentioned with the tens of thousands of subscribers and big teams, I admire them and I'm happy for them, but I don't want to be like them. A business that size with that many employees and that much complexity would not serve my goals. And I'll let you in on a little secret: my profit margin is higher than many of them. Their revenue numbers might be a lot bigger than mine, but several of them wish they had my profits.

You get to create your path. Believe in yourself and your dream. Keep your why in mind as you make decisions about growing your business. No one says you have to keep going just for the sake of it. You're in control; you're in the driver's seat. Get honest with yourself: What do you *really* want?

Action Steps

1. It's a big question, but it's time to answer: What do you want now?

2. How big is big enough? Have you thought through how big you want to grow? How does that work with the lifestyle you envision?

3. Get in a community. Join a mastermind, start a group chat with some biz besties, whatever it takes. Don't go it alone.

CONCLUSION

YOU'RE NOT ALONE

A few months ago, I took my family on an amazing beach vacation. We had an absolute blast, and it was the kind of trip that gave me the bone-deep rest I'd been so desperately needing after a busy season of business. On the last night, I walked down to the beach by myself for a bit and watched the sunset. I know this sounds like something out of a movie, cheesy even, but I got deep into my thoughts and had some realizations.

Years ago, when I started my business, I was a young mother of two children with just a dream. Not a dream to have a multimillion-dollar business—I couldn't even conceive of that yet. It would have seemed completely out of reach. My only dream was to make a living doing something I loved. We were often living paycheck to paycheck, and it was tough. I figured, if I was going to struggle and work this hard for not a ton of money, I may as well do it for myself and enjoy what I do.

For 18 months I plugged along, clocking 15-hour days, staying up after the kids went to bed, and getting up at 4 A.M. before they got up again, just so I could keep my side gig afloat before I worked up the courage to quit my full-time job. Quitting my full-time job was the scariest thing I ever did. I wouldn't have said it this way then, but in hindsight I know the only reason I was able to go for it was because something deep inside knew I could do it.

I sacrificed so much for what I have today. There were years when I didn't take a single day off, missed important life events, didn't go on vacation, and stress ate tubs of ice cream in the fetal position. There were many, many days when I went to bed thinking there was no way I could keep going but somehow woke up in the morning and did. And I would do it all over again, every single time.

The thing is, I don't want that for you. Of course, I want you to have the business of your dreams. What I don't want is for you to miss anything or struggle unnecessarily. Entrepreneurship is hard—I'll be the first to tell you that. You'll likely have some late nights and early mornings. You'll cry and doubt yourself and make mistakes. But the reason I do everything I do now for my students, for you, is because I want you to do it better than me. You can work hard and have a life you love. You can be a fun and present parent and a boss CEO. Your business can work right into the life you want to have. I've given you a playbook to skip so many of the mistakes I made and do it better and faster.

Take to heart everything I've taught you in these pages. I know a lot of it is tactical and practical. But the passion behind it is all about this: financial freedom, loving what you do, *getting* to go to work instead of *having* to go to work, time to do what you want, having options for your family. That is what's available for you, if you take action.

My subscription box business was the key to everything I have now. As I looked out at the sunset on a vacation that cost me over a month's worth of my old salary, thinking back on the weekend I just had with my family, the overwhelming feeling was gratitude. It was all worth it because it brought me here.

You can have the life and business of your dreams, and I'm more convinced than ever that the best way to do that is through a subscription box business. Handpicking out gifts for people every single month and making a great living off it? What would be better than that? We're literally delivering joy and making money.

The last piece of advice I want to leave you with is this: you don't have to do it alone. Every turning point in my business—the art studio, opening the store, creating the subscription business, stepping into my role as CEO, starting my course and membership and mastermind—all happened because of community. Go find your people. There is a community of fellow subscription box business owners out there waiting to welcome you with open arms. We are the most fun people on the Internet, I swear. You can get where you want to go so much faster and easier if you do it with others.

I am so grateful to have been a part of your journey. My family has always been my deepest why driving my business. But a close second is you, the subscription box hopeful who is just a few months away from changing their life. So, I'll say it one more time: you can do this. Take the next step. I'll be here every step of the way, cheering you on. I can't wait to watch you shine.

ACKNOWLEDGMENTS

The journey to finish this book was completely out of my comfort zone. That self-doubt I talked about so much throughout the book definitely crept up on me during the book writing process. It's taken over a year to get here from when we wrote the very first words of the proposal.

This book was unexpected and would not have happened if it weren't for Stu McLaren. In so many ways, he was the pivotal part of this book existing. It all started one December day when Stu asked me to be a part of a charity event in Arizona. There I met with some other amazing entrepreneurs as we prepped to give our industry predictions live for an audience all over the world. At that event was Stu's good friend, Reid Tracy, Hay House CEO. As we spent the day together, Stu was talking about his upcoming book and implied that I should have a book, too. I laughed and said, "I don't need a book." I am not a writer, and at that time, I didn't enjoy reading books. My mind couldn't ever settle enough to really comprehend what I was reading, so I felt like it was a waste of my precious time.

Soon the room broke down all the reasons writing a book would be great for me. Reid jumped in and said, let's talk. Stu has been my coach and mentor for over five years. I am incredibly grateful to have him as a friend and mentor. You don't always align with everyone you meet, but when you find that alignment, lean in and open yourself up to all the opportunities that come your way. Reid trusted Stu's judgment and welcomed me to the Hay House family immediately.

Terrified and second guessing what I had just gotten myself into, the first person I reached out to was Marilee Haynes. She'd been on my team for a little over a year and always took my words and made them sound better and more polished. I knew instantly I wanted her to help me write this book. Little did I know, she was actually an author herself. She's super modest and had never shared that with me. Marilee combed through my membership and course materials, podcast episodes, blog articles, interviews, and put together a fabulous manuscript. One that took months of blood, sweat, and tears—many tears, from both of us. This process was not easy and left us vulnerable along the way. She was an incredible person to lean on during this process. She knew me and I trusted her with my words.

We added in Liz Morrow, who I can't thank enough for coming along and being an incredible support system to Marilee and me. Liz was so patient and cared for this book as if it were her own. It was important for me to have the people working on this book that felt the importance of the content and the connections I had with my students, and Liz was right there every step of the way.

There are more amazing people who helped make this book exist. There is so much in life that contributed to my story and made this possible. To my Mom and Dad, Joan and Paul Yowell, who helped me believe I could be anything I set my mind to be. I am the creative entrepreneur in our family of five and although they couldn't relate to my ambitions, they always supported me in anything I wanted to do. My siblings, Nathan and Kelsey, inspire me daily. They are passionate about their careers and always supportive of mine.

Although I wake up every day loving what I do, there is nothing that makes me happier than my kids, Jackson and Addison. They've known this entrepreneurial Mom their entire life. They probably think it's what all normal moms do. They've swept floors, cleaned windows, folded boxes, helped schlep my products to shows and jumped in to help any way they could. My son jokes and calls me "small town famous." Someday he will understand the impact I've had on so many other women finding their way along their entrepreneurial path. My daughter is curious and asked a lot of questions. I'm not sure where their paths will lead, but I know I will be there to support them with anything they want to do.

To my amazing friends and family that have been my cheerleaders and biggest supporters. Sometimes we find that the people closest to us are the least supportive of us, but I am grateful to have the opposite in my life. Of course, Quincy, who never doubted me, and who always let me dream the bigger dream, no matter how far away it was.

To the Creative Club, my long-lost sisters, my biz besties, the ones that always empower me, lift me up, and care deeply for me both personally and professionally. Christie, Tamara, Heidi, Kasey, Gretchen, Cindy, and Brandie; you have been the most priceless gifts in my life that I never knew I needed. Business is personal, period. Having people in your life that understand both parts of you are incredibly powerful for your growth.

To my peers and mentors, the hardest part is that there have been so many people along the way that have been a part of my business journey, I am afraid I am going to miss someone and I can't stomach that, so I'll say this. If you've jumped on a Zoom call to help me through a problem, if you've sat on a couch with me binge eating chips while strategizing, if you've Voxed with me at all hours of the day or night, I am talking to you. The people that believed in me more than I believed in myself most days. Thank you for seeing me for who I am, thank you for helping me through the problem at hand, thank you for just being a person I could lean on.

To the entire team, both in person and remote. This book wouldn't have happened without you. Amber, Jolene, Joey, Lauren, LJ, Allison, Marilee, Alison, Keri, Kelsey, Mat, Marissa, Gretchen, and Sarah H., you've been a constant source of inspiration, dedication, and support throughout this journey. Not knowing where the path was going to take us, but always up for the ride, and even driving the bus most of the time. I am so grateful and appreciative of each of you. The best is yet to come.

I've dedicated this book to the Launch Your Box community. I am a better person because of you. You've inspired me in ways that you can't possibly imagine. With every story I've shared in this book, there are hundreds more. Hundreds of incredible humans taking the next step to becoming an entrepreneur and building a life they've dreamt of. A life of freedom, in whatever way you want that freedom, because it's yours to choose. Never stop believing you have that choice. Never give up on yourself. Keep pushing forward and overcoming obstacles in your path. Because there will be obstacles, some bigger than others. Keep reminding yourself you are capable, you are worthy, and you are inspiring someone else. Go build the life you want, *One Box at a Time.*

ABOUT THE AUTHOR

Sarah Williams started her entrepreneurial journey in 2013 with a brick-and-mortar retail store that quickly became a thriving local business. The desire to provide her most loyal customers with an exclusive, VIP-style experience led her to launch a subscription box in 2017, despite having little knowledge of that business. In 2023, Sarah's company made it onto the Inc. 5000 list of fastest-growing companies in America.

Sarah dug in and learned all the things she needed to know in order to launch and grow a subscription box business. The result? A seven-figure business dedicated to surprising and delighting thousands of subscribers each month. The consistent, recurring revenue generated by her subscription boxes transformed Sarah's business, and her life.

The same desire to serve that led Sarah to start her subscription box then led her to teach other product-based entrepreneurs how to start their own subscription box businesses. Sarah and her team work with thousands of subscription box entrepreneurs every day within her two signature programs, Launch Your Box and Scale Your Box, as well as inside her Elevate Mastermind.

Sarah delights in watching Launch Your Box members start, launch, and grow their own subscription box businesses. Being part of helping other women reach their goals inspires her to continue to provide them with the tools and support they need to reach levels of success they never imagined possible.

Through her memberships and top-ranked podcast, the *Launch Your Box Podcast,* Sarah helps people realize the dreams they have for their own subscription box businesses. Sarah's practical, action-oriented teaching style not only provides subscription box owners with the tools and knowledge to achieve their business goals, but the inspiration and motivation to believe they can do it. As the owner of two seven-figure businesses, Sarah is frequently sought out as an expert in the subscription box industry, regularly appearing on podcasts, industry publications, and on stage at live industry events.

Despite being called "The Subscription Box Queen" by some of her mentors and peers, Sarah is much more likely to be seen on the sidelines of her kids' sporting events than wearing a crown around her north Texas town. Fueled by caffeine, Sarah happily fills her two favorite roles: successful business owner and mom of two teenagers.

www.launchyourbox.com

Hay House Titles of Related Interest

We hope you enjoyed this Hay House book. If you'd like to receive our online catalog featuring additional information on Hay House books and products, or if you'd like to find out more about the Hay Foundation, please contact:

Hay House, Inc., P.O. Box 5100, Carlsbad, CA 92018-5100
(760) 431-7695 or (800) 654-5126
(760) 431-6948 (fax) or (800) 650-5115 (fax)
www.hayhouse.com® • www.hayfoundation.org

———

Published in Australia by: Hay House Australia Pty. Ltd.,
18/36 Ralph St., Alexandria NSW 2015
Phone: 612-9669-4299 • *Fax:* 612-9669-4144
www.hayhouse.com.au

Published in the United Kingdom by: Hay House UK, Ltd.,
The Sixth Floor, Watson House, 54 Baker Street, London W1U 7BU
Phone: +44 (0)20 3927 7290 • *Fax:* +44 (0)20 3927 7291
www.hayhouse.co.uk

Published in India by: Hay House Publishers India,
Muskaan Complex, Plot No. 3, B-2, Vasant Kunj, New Delhi 110 070
Phone: 91-11-4176-1620 • *Fax:* 91-11-4176-1630
www.hayhouse.co.in

———

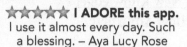